ALBION'S DREAM

ROGER NORMAN

THE SUNDIAL PRESS

ALBION'S DREAM

First published in a hardback edition by Faber and Faber in 1990

Reissued by The Sundial Press in 2012 and 2018

THE SUNDIAL PRESS
Sundial House
The Sheeplands, Sherborne, Dorset DT9 4BS

www.sundialpress.co.uk

Copyright © Roger Norman

Roger Norman has asserted his moral right to be identified as the author of this work in accordance with the Copyright, Designs and Patents Act, 1988

A CIP catalogue record for this book is available from the British Library

Front cover image: © Alan Baker

Cover Design: Frank Kibblewhite

All rights reserved. This publication may not be reproduced, stored in a retrieval system or transmitted in any form or by any means, electronic, mechanical, photocopying, recording or otherwise, without prior permission in writing from the publishers.

ISBN 978-1-908274-66-3

Contents

1.	The Name of the Game	1
2.	The Merchant, the King and the Queen	15
3.	The Friendly Hangman	26
4.	Pellinore and Puck	44
5.	The Barrow and The Dome	65
6.	The Dungeon	79
7.	Doctor Death	93
8.	Merlin	110
9.	Galahad	135
10.	Hod	150
11.	The Camp and The Dole	169
12.	The Battle for the Rings	184
13.	The Fall of The King	195
14.	The Giant's Grave	216

CHAPTER ONE

THE NAME OF THE GAME

IT took me a long journey, two thousand miles, to learn to dig a post hole and to hoe a long row, to plant a tree, to kill a chicken and to build a stone wall, but the soil here is not like Wessex soils, the trees are stunted, the rivers run dry and the hillsides are clad in thick, coarse scrub covering the ancient conformations.

My family is here, my house is here, but it is too far from Wessex. Say the word hill, and I think of the grassy flanks of Hambledon; say tree and I think of towering beeches and the doomed elms of Dorset hedgerows; say river and I think of the Dorset Stour, low and clear and ice-fringed, or high and muddy, or summered with green reed banks and dragonflies. Say the word home and I think of a particular deep bend of that river where my mother must have caught me up and whispered me some love magic – or perhaps it was where I landed my first pike.

But if the Blackmoor Vale is my first love, I have lived, too, among the hills to the west of it and in a museum town to the north of it, and beyond the great, wet flatlands of Sedgemoor, at the foot of the Quantocks, lies the little village of Turnworth where my father's family come from and where my uncle had a farm. For this small farm and for the rambling Somersetshire farmhouse I

THE NAME OF THE GAME

have nourished a romantic affection from my earliest years. I used to make maps, plans and charts of those acres, listing numbers of cattle to be raised, quantities of barley, potatoes and apples which I would one day harvest with my own hands, and even details of the dogs I would keep and where my shotgun would hang on the wall.

There were rooms in the old farmhouse which I never saw used and which smelt of a past that held an extraordinary fascination for me; little windows where unknown ancestors had sat on autumn evenings and watched the mallard flying down to feed on the stubble; old leather-lined bookcases with books that no one had handled for fifty years; dust that no one bothered to remove, piles of candlewax in unlikely corners; huge chamber pots and cracked basins, and everywhere a great generosity of space. There was an enormous bathroom where the bath occupied a tiny fraction of the room at one end, and the loo stood raised on a platform like a throne at the other – a room where for half the year you could never feel quite warm except by vigorous ablutions – and a narrow pantry in which the only furniture was a long, scrubbed table, always empty, and some massive marble shelves. Outside there was a big lawn hardly walked on, flowerbeds hardly looked at, a vegetable garden which always produced too much, a vast horse chestnut with enough conkers to satisfy the needs of a whole village of boys, a second lawn that nobody ever sat on, and the poignant smells of animals and harvests of a bygone age.

And amidst all this lived my uncle as quietly and modestly as if

THE NAME OF THE GAME

he didn't own the place, but was simply comfortable to be able to stay there as long as he pleased, comfortable without luxuries or improvements or pretensions, enjoying the absolute familiarity of his physical surroundings — the same huge teacup at every breakfast (while another thirty looked on) and two springer spaniels called Spot and Nip. When Spot died another Spot came, when Nip died there was another Nip.

There also lived with him an elderly spinster called Em Sharp who was the true guardian of the place and of the memories of the family, my father's family, who had lived there. The farmhouse never got any cleaner under her care, but it never got any dirtier either. In fact she was determined that nothing should change, and nothing did. She was a very determined woman, Em Sharp, hard and unimaginative as a chisel, but doting on her 'boy', Uncle Jack, keeping a hawklike eye on his movements and intentions, so that when, finally, he did want to make some changes in the house — at a time in his early fifties when he began to think that he might marry, or that the dust was getting too thick on the china while everything around him was suddenly and seriously modernising — Miss Sharp had to be removed to a nearby home for old people, together with the best of her things, gleaned from a lifetime at Turnworth.

I don't suppose she could ever quite forgive Jack for thus disposing of her, yet deep down she must always have known that should he marry or otherwise radically alter the style of his life, her term at Turnworth would come to an end. Perhaps it was this

THE NAME OF THE GAME

fear that made her such a demanding and pernickety housekeeper. She died before Jack moved into his new home and married his wife, before he exchanged every last thing of his material possessions down to teacup and coal scuttle, surprising me with the ease and pleasure he felt in his spanking new surroundings, cheerfully condemning the old place, its draughts and drips and emptiness. He didn't even seem upset when the new M5 motorway slashed through the middle of his acres, ruining for ever the peace of the park. He had been well warned, he said, and adequately compensated, and the horrendous summer bottlenecks around Bridgewater were a thing of the past.

It was the motorway, and the sale of the old house, rather than my uncle's marriage, which put an end to my own pleasant fantasies of inheriting Turnworth Park.

While I was a boy, my father used to take me for visits to Jack. Sometimes these were family outings but more often it was just my father and myself with our guns and gun cases and cartridge belts and brandy flask and a change of socks and thick jumpers and that special atmosphere between us that my father generated when at his ease. He would drive fast and surely through the twisting lanes that led from the Blackmoor Vale over the Sherborne ridges and down to Sedgemoor. It was only an hour's drive and yet it felt a long way from our family home and its daily routines. My father shed his role as paterfamilias and seemed to grow younger and more carefree the closer we approached the

THE NAME OF THE GAME

pastures of his boyhood, following the withy lined curves of the Sedgemoor waterways. For the space of a day my father was more like a brother. In all our visits I do not remember a cross word passing between the three of us – my father, my uncle and myself.

Better still were the times, as I grew older, when I went to stay with Jack on my own. I followed him on his work around the farm, or explored the empty rooms of the farmhouse. One day – I was twelve years old – it was raining cats and dogs and Jack had taken the car to drive into Bridgewater on business. Left to my own devices, I visited the dogs and the battery of young chicks, watched Em Sharp for a while as she prepared lunch, then made my way upstairs into the most largest and most remote of the empty rooms where there was a big leather-lined bookcase that had attracted my curiosity. Its contents were mostly unknown to me: Victorian novels and books of travels, together with some more recent fiction, Dornford Yates and Mary Webb and Henry Williamson.

I pulled out some of the books, glancing idly at the contents, and then, as I went to return one of them to its place, my eye was caught by something in the dark recesses of the shelf. I reached in and drew it out. It was a large red dice, but like no other dice I had ever seen.

I took it to the window to inspect it. Each face held a symbol: a cross, a tower, a sword, a broken circle, something that looked like a pillar of stone, and a skull. It was obvious that the dice had been fashioned by hand, for I could even make out the tiny blade marks and none of the faces was precisely even.

THE NAME OF THE GAME

As I sat and puzzled over the symbols, it dawned on me that the dice ought to belong to a game of some kind. So I returned to the bookcase to make a thorough search.

I looked behind every book and used my hand to sweep out the shallow gap under the bottom shelf. There must have been ten years' worth of assorted debris under there, but nothing that gave me any clue to the mysterious dice. Finally I began to edge the entire bookcase away from the wall. It was extremely heavy and it took me some time to get it out far enough to look behind. There was a thick network of cobwebs and dust. I thought for a moment of an old rat holed up in there, dismissed the thought and plunged my hand into the gap.

There was something there, a flat box. It was covered with grime and falling apart. Opening it, I found a board, counters, cards, and a number of little figures. I smeared away the dirt from the lid and made out the title. *Albion's Dream*, it said.

At that moment I heard Em Sharp's voice coming up the stairs.

"Edward. EDWARD," she called. "What on earth are you up to in there?" She must have heard the bookcase being moved. The door opened. "What was that scraping noise. You be careful..." She broke off abruptly.

It took her a few seconds to work out what I was doing, then she leapt towards me. I had no idea the old biddy could move so fast. If I hadn't been so excited by my discovery and fired by a sense of possessiveness for what I had found, she might have grabbed it from me there and then and this tale would never have been written. But I was faster than she, and as she stumbled a little, I swept up the box, circled her nimbly and ran to the door. There I paused to see her reaction. Her old face was flushed and angry.

"Give me that immediately, Edward." I drew back cautiously. "That box is mine. It's nothing to do with you. It belongs to me."

She came forward with a frightening intensity, her hand reaching out for the box. I hesitated. If it really was hers, I had no right…But a stronger sense of justice broke out in me. I had found it by my own efforts. For the time being, at least, it was mine. I headed rapidly for the stairs and skipped down them two by two, hearing her shout after me. I opened the front door and ran out into the pouring rain. A minute later I was sitting breathlessly in the big barn, concealed among the bales of straw. I waited for a while, but it seemed that Em Sharp had given up the chase.

I took the board out of the box and laid it open in front of me. There were five concentric circles drawn in black ink, and each ring so formed was shaded a different colour, apparently depicting a different landscape. The outer circle was grey, the second red, then green, blue and finally black at the centre. At certain points were marked castles or fortresses, each distinguished by a heavy symbol, the same symbols that I had seen on the red dice. The design was so careful that it took me some time to realise that the whole thing had been drawn by hand, in crayons and inks, and when I looked again at the lid of the box, I noticed that the title, too, had been written by hand in black ink. Around it were drawn seven rosettes, as if of brass – the sort of thing you might expect to find decorating the hilt of a sword.

Apart from the board itself, the box contained a number of amber-coloured beads, some tiny figurines, apparently representing different characters, and two packs of cards. There was also a large white dice, this one marked in the usual way, from one to six. It was all very carefully and lavishly fashioned – it reminded me of my father's Mah Jong set. The cards in particular were highly elaborate, each one inked and coloured by hand. The same seven rosettes showed on their backs. I picked up the bulkier of the two packs and turned over the top card.

It was Tyson!

There was no doubt about it. They were Tyson's features that leapt out at me from the face on the card. It shocked me deeply, his sudden appearance in front of me, among the straw bales of Turnworth.

Tyson was the headmaster of my school and the very devil of a passionate tyrant, full of order and ire. In the days and weeks that followed I could never again see his whole face there on this card, but the eyes remained unmistakable, watching piercingly from behind thick lenses. The legend under the character read: 'The Friendly Hangman'.

'Friendly!' I thought. 'Tyson's not friendly.' And yet this was not altogether true. He could be friendly, Tyson, when he had a mind to. He could turn on you his own brand of cheerful and physical charm. It did not occur to me, however, to wonder whether or not he could play the role of hangman.

THE NAME OF THE GAME

I started to look through the rest of the cards, but the sound of Jack's motor reached me from the bottom of the drive as the car swung round the deep corner under the conker tree. I peered out from my perch. The rain had stopped and Em Sharp was running in my direction. She saw my head above the straw as I hastily packed the game into its box and began to push it between two of the bales.

"Edward. Quickly," she called from the doorway. I watched her suspiciously. "No, don't worry. I'm not coming to take it. Hide it and don't say anything to Jack."

She placed such a curious emphasis on this instruction that I did not think of disobeying. I understood that we had become accomplices.

After lunch Jack took me over to the park to help feed some cattle. While we were busy with this I suddenly felt anxious about the safety of my game.

"Why don't I go and bring the dogs?" I said to Jack. "They'll enjoy the walk." I turned to hurry back to the house.

"No, don't bring them. They bother the bullocks. We'll finish here and you can take them out later. You can take your gun, too, if you like, and see if there are any duck on the pond behind the orchard."

He didn't often favour me with such invitations, but it was wasted on me now in my overriding impatience to get back to the barn. When at last we had finished with the cattle, I hurried on in front of him. "To check if my gun's clean," I called over my shoulder.

THE NAME OF THE GAME

My fears were quickly confirmed. There was no sign of the box in its hiding place, and I could see the track between the bales where the old lady must have pulled herself up.

I had to wait before I could go in pursuit of the game. Jack had returned and he watched me while I prepared my gun and took out the dogs.

"One will do," he said. "Take Spot."

So I took Spot and we walked through the orchard. Usually when I had my gun in my hands, I started at blackbirds and my heart missed a beat at the sound of a snipe. But now my thoughts were elsewhere and I allowed Spot to run on ahead. He put up a flight of little teal while I was still far out of range, but I put the gun to my shoulder and fired a despairing shot after them. The report shattered the silence like a pointless announcement of my clumsiness to the listening world. I sat for a while among the reeds, more to satisfy Jack's expectations of me than in the hope of the teal returning. I fondled the dog's ears and thought of the game in Em Sharp's possession. Would she burn it? Would I be able to capture it back?

Jack was watching grimly over the gate of the orchard as I trudged up the hill.

"There's no point in firing at teal seventy yards away," he said sternly. "You're only likely to wing a bird, and it'll get down in the water among the reeds where the dog can't smell it and die slowly during the night. That's not sport. And," he continued emphatically, "don't allow my dog to run wild. It's a bad habit."

THE NAME OF THE GAME

Teatime had always been a deep and quiet pleasure in Jack's company, with the fire blazing and the T.V. on, with plenty of toast or crumpets and thick yellow butter never too hard or too soft, and chocolate biscuits and cake and Jack urging me merrily to eat more, to eat it all – but on this occasion it was a sad affair. Jack was irritated with me, and I with myself. I couldn't think of another time when we had been so out of sorts with each other. I respected him greatly and was always careful of his opinion. He in his turn was at ease in his kindly but avuncular dealings with me, appreciating, I think, the presence of a quiet and youthful shadow, one which did not require him to change his routines or depart from the standards of a lifetime.

Later it did not seem a coincidence to me that this unhappy breach in my friendship with Jack followed immediately my discovery of the game. At that moment, however, I was too impatient even to stick around until the atmosphere mellowed. I mumbled an excuse while the teapot was still good and hot under its cosy, and went in search of Em Sharp.

She was in her room. Although leading off from the front hall, and therefore only a couple of dozen steps from where Jack sat in front of his fire, Em Sharp's room was alien territory to me – I had been in there only once before with my father. I remember it crammed with unlikely ornament, small and dim like the old lady in her solitude.

When I knocked at the door, she answered immediately as if she had been expecting me. "Come in," she said, "and close the door." She didn't seem angry, but covert and uneasy. She went and listened by the door a moment before pushing me to a chair. My eyes scanned the room for a sign of the game.

"No, you won't find it," she said. "Sit down. I told you the game was mine so you needn't bother looking for it. It has a…" She hesitated. "It has a sentimental value for me, and I don't want it interfered with."

"But you must have lost it years ago," I said. "And anyway, I won't mess it up, I just want to look at it. It seems an interesting game," I finished weakly. In truth I was surprised at how passionately I wanted to get hold of it again. Perhaps this made me canny.

"You looked at it, of course." She was watching me fiercely. "*All* of it?" There was some particular weight to this question which put me on my guard.

"Yes, all of it," I said.

"What, even the…," but she stopped short.

"Even the what?" I asked.

"Oh no. Oh no. You saw only the game, didn't you? The game by itself means nothing. Without the instructions, I mean."

"I didn't see any instructions."

"No, you saw no instructions. Well, well, you should be glad. Have some fudge." She reached up for a large box of fudge from the mantelpiece.

"Yes, thankyou. No—wait. I saw more than the game."

"You did?" Her eyes narrowed, the fudge was withdrawn in mid air. "What exactly did you see?"

"I saw someone I know."

Now she was really interested. I watched her throw a quick glance up towards the top shelf of her dresser. The game was there, then.

"Someone you know? Whatever do you mean?"

But I was convinced I was on the right track.

"I recognised a card. The face on a card. It was the face of someone I know."

"Which card?" She was almost hissing.

"The Friendly Hangman. It was my headmaster."

She fell silent, but continued to eye me closely while apparently deliberating with herself. After a moment she got up and reached painfully to the top shelf. From under some papers and a pile of napkins she drew out the game. I noticed that the battered edges of the box had been repaired.

"Then you have started to play," she said. Her tone of voice took me by surprise. There was an excitement in it, as of complicity, but there was something else, too. Something wary or frightened.

"And when you have started to play, you must be allowed to continue." She sat down heavily with the box on her lap. "I'm going to hand this over to you," she said. "It isn't mine and never was. It belonged to your father and perhaps it was destined to come to you, but I'm sure he would not have chosen to give it to you. I wanted to do as he and Jack would have wished. When I took it from the barn, I came here to burn it." She was talking quietly now, almost to herself. "But then I had to have a last look at it, and I saw Will's letter, and I read it and remembered the game. All the games, all the extraordinary games. And I thought, I'll keep it for a bit, I won't destroy it yet. And perhaps I was waiting for you to come, perhaps I really did want you to have read the letter."

"You mean the letter containing the instructions?" I asked.

"Well, yes. The instructions and the warning. Take heed of the warning, Edward, and don't ever, ever tell Jack you have the game. And if he should discover it, tell him where you found it, but don't mention me at all. Don't mention my name." She seemed really anxious now, and suddenly in a hurry for me to leave. "I'll leave the game under your pillow when I turn back your covers this evening. From then on it's in your charge. But be careful, Edward, and pay attention to the letter."

CHAPTER TWO

THE MERCHANT, THE KING AND THE QUEEN

IN an envelope at the bottom of the box were several sheets of paper in my father's handwriting. 'To whoever should wish to play *Albion's Dream*,' the text began. And it continued:

"Perhaps I ought to have destroyed this game because of the harm of which it is capable. And yet I cannot help feeling that our troubles stemmed more from Jack's exaggerated reactions than from the game itself. After all, what is it but a board, some cards and some counters? My own father had played it, he told me, and he had never mentioned any curious effects. He passed it on to me without a warning, just the simple instructions. All he told me that it was not to be played outside the family. It was a family inheritance, he said, and I should take care of it as he had done and his father before him.

He didn't tell me anything of its history, and later when I would have asked him, it was too late. He mentioned only that his father had made the game and drawn the cards and designed the board, but I remember his adding that the dice were much older, he did not know how old. They should be looked after with especial care, he said. None of this roused my curiosity – I just thought it was an ordinary game with some family history attached to it.

For a while Jack and I played without any great surprises. It was a good game for winter evenings. The only odd thing to begin with was the way in which the Merchant kept turning up to me. I drew him nearly every time and he was very lucky for me. He led me unhesitatingly to the fortresses and he had an uncanny skill in battles and encounters. Even the warriors in Jack's hand seemed unable to stand up to him.

Then one night I dreamed of him. He was standing outside the smouldering ruins of his factory. Workers were standing around him, silent and shocked. "Fun tomorrow," he was shouting. "Fun tomorrow."

Then he turned suddenly towards me. He said nothing, but his gaze was full of a friendly warmth. His features were no longer those of the Merchant card although his eyes had the same clever twinkle. When I looked at the card the next morning, it did not much resemble the man in my dream, but the eyes were the same.

I was seventeen at the time, head of my school, captain of the rugby and cricket teams. My father had decided that I would become a solicitor, a prospect that gave me no great pleasure, but I was used to following obediently the paths that had been chosen for me. One day at school, the headmaster sent for me.

"I would like you to meet a friend of mine," he said. And there in the chair beside him was the Merchant of my dream. A sunburnt face, a prominent brow and nose and those tricky, twinkling eyes.

I was on my best behaviour before a distinguished friend of my headmaster's. I did not allow myself to be discomfited by the coincidence of the man's appearance. For what else could it be but coincidence?

"This is Henry Ness," the headmaster said. We shook hands.

When we were left alone, Henry Ness put the question to me: "Have you ever thought of commerce as a career?"

"No," I answered truthfully.

"Why not?"

"Because my father wants me to be a solicitor. And anyway, I think commerce is immoral."

"In that case, why don't you join it and do something to change it?" he said.

His eyes were shining and the force of his attention was magnetic. If he had chosen with the utmost care, he could not have found a more attractive challenge for me. That was Henry's skill. He could read character with a sure instinct. From that moment the lines of my future were irrevocably changed."

I knew the rest of that story, or the gist of it. When my father left school the following year, Henry took him into his firm. Under his guidance my father built what everyone regarded as a conspicuously successful career in the world of business. And I do not believe that he ever lost sight of his initial motive for choosing the course that he did.

Henry later became my godfather and I, too, became the recipient of his charm and of the air of cheerful success that he radiated. I also heard the story of how, in 1941, just after a huge contract had been signed with the Chinese government, his factory in South London was destroyed by bombs, how he had rushed to the site wearing his pyjamas under his overcoat and how he had dismissed the disaster with a wave of the hand. "Fun tomorrow," he had said. It was his favourite line.

The letter went on: "I still treated the card, the dream and Henry's appearance as no more than an unusual coincidence. I did not tell Jack of it. But there was a new development. Perhaps I was partly to blame. I began to attach a particular significance to the Merchant card. I was irritated if it fell to Jack, although this happened rarely enough. In some way I began to associate my future success in commerce with the game and the part played therein by the Merchant. I concentrated on the acquisition of the amber tokens, often turning down the chance of approaching closer to the centre of the board. I would hole up in one of my favourite fortresses and amass tokens by daring raids and surprise attacks. Jack would proceed doggedly towards the centre.

When I say I was partly responsible for what happened next, I mean that Jack's earnestness was perhaps provoked by my own. He, too, developed a favourite card, one of the most powerful and difficult cards of the whole game: the Christ card.

THE MERCHANT, THE KING AND THE QUEEN

Now I should explain that Christ is merely one of the three mages, and that his power in the game is conditional and tricky to employ. If played at the wrong time, he is easily bypassed or stripped of his power. Only close to the centre does his value become supreme. My strategy was to allow Jack to depend on the Christ card, to prevent him reaching a position where he could use it. He became obsessed with the possession of this card and, true to form, it nearly always fell to him. My strategy was largely successful because the power of the Merchant is greater in the outer rings and the action can be prevented from approaching the centre by control of the fortresses. This in turn is decided by the warrior cards and I was quite reckless in using up my warriors to gain fortresses and close up the passes. Jack understood my strategy but he insisted that the proper aim was not control but progress towards the centre. Sometimes he would collect all three of the mages, only to be denied the opportunity to use them. Occasionally he was the winner, but far more often it was I.

He became increasingly serious during the playing of the games. Once he lost three warriors at one fortress and was close to tears.

"That's life," I said.

"It's not. It's not," he shouted back at me. "It's not life, it's only a game. Life isn't like that at all."

The strength of his outburst showed me that, on the contrary, the game had become very close to life for him. Too close.

We used to play in the big room upstairs. Em Sharp would light the fire for us there, and after we had finished our homework, we would sit and play by the window overlooking the park. Em would stay and watch us whenever she could. She never said anything, but she never missed a move either. There was no electricity in the room and we played by the light of an old brass oil lamp which we turned up as the daylight faded.

One day we couldn't get the log fire to burn. The wood was wet or green and the room had filled with smoke. The wick on the oil lamp needed trimming, and the flame was restless, blackening the glass. Jack, for once, was in a strong position. He had Christ and Merlin, and the King was turned up to him. He was in the Third Kingdom and needed only to find a guide in order to gain the Fourth. At this point he drew the Death card, threw the red dice and got the Skull, the worst of all options. He now had to throw the white dice, and threw a six. In one blow he lost Christ, Merlin, his two warriors, the Judge and the King. The game was over for him.

It was an unprecedented stroke of misfortune. In all our games Death had only intervened marginally and now he had literally cleared the board. Without a word, Jack ran from the room. I stayed to pack the game away and coax a little life into the fire. A few minutes later I heard a kind of shout from below and the sound of footsteps hurriedly climbing the stairs. The door flew open and Jack stood there pale and trembling.

"Don't take on so," I told him. "It's just a game."

He was crying with fury and fright.

"It's not just a game. Don't you understand, it's real, it's evil." He buried his face in his hands.

"What is it? What's happened?"

"It's father, he's had an accident with the horse. He's dying, Will, he's dying."

It was true. Our father died that night. His back was broken. He had been returning late from the market, drunk, as always on market days, and his horse had thrown him on the road outside the 'Black Swan'. They had carried him into the inn, but he never regained consciousness.

All that spring and summer the game stayed on its shelf. I would have preferred never to play again. The ugly coincidence of the death of the King—I still treated it as coincidence and do now, for what else could it have been? But it also frightened me, as did Jack's absolute conviction that the game was something more than a game.

Yet it was he who insisted that we play again. In the meantime I had moved to London but I had ten days holiday over Christmas. Jack had virtually taken over the running of the farm. He was only sixteen, but he had started to look a lot older. The death of my father had put an end to his education and he was destined to work on the farm. He had never voiced any objection to this and I assumed that he was happy. He had met a girl from a neighbouring farm and had fallen in love with her. On my first evening home, a few days before Christmas 1933, he suggested getting out the game. At first I refused.

"You can't refuse me," he said. "Don't you see where I am left after that last game? I am stranded with no cards in my hands, no tokens. You are blessed by success at every step."

"Only through my own hard work."

"Yes, you work, but doesn't it take luck and guidance and a little money in your pocket? Don't you think I work too? Look at my hands." He held them out, scarred and callused and scored with dirt. I looked at my own, white and soft.

"But what does the game have to do with it?"

"Don't you understand anything? Weren't you here when father died? Didn't you see the Merchant appearing time and time again in your hand? And wasn't I always losing my players and my tokens?"

I felt a pang of sympathy for my brother. I loved him, you see, and still do, for all the difference in our temperaments and in the lines of our fate. I agreed to play, but I insisted it should be for the last time.

I made up my mind to lose the game – without his noticing, to waste my opportunities and to fail to exploit my pieces.

At my suggestion we played in the morning. It was raining hard, slanting from the west over the moor, one of those days when the westerly tasted of the salt of the distant coasts. I waited for Jack, standing at the window of the big room. The fire blazed healthily. I felt that we could, this morning, lay the ghost of the game.

As I waited, my eye caught sight of a girl coming down the path from the park. She was slim and fair and wore gum boots too big for her. It was wet and slippery at the stile beyond the lawn, but she went at it fast, anyway, and vaulted it with the ease of one used to ponies and fences and mud. She cleared the stile, but her boots slipped as she landed and she half ran, half slid into the big bramble bush. She was scratched and muddied from her fall but she leapt instantly to her feet and threw a great smile to the rainy sky. She must have caught a glimpse of me then, because she looked quickly over at the window where I was standing, with the smile still on her lips, and that was how I first saw her.

While I watched, Jack came into the room. He moved to the window beside me and saw who it was I was watching. He blushed.

"That's Sue," he said.

I had guessed it.

"She's very pretty," I said.

She was.

But I had not guessed what would follow. Jack wanted Sue to be there for the game. For his luck, he explained. I reminded him that the game was not to be played outside the family.

"That doesn't apply to onlookers," he said. I said that I thought it did, but really it was that I didn't want Sue at the game. I'm not sure why.

"What about Em, then?" he said. "She watches."

"Em's different. She's like family."

"Well, Sue's like family too."

I hadn't understood how serious he was about her. I had to agree to her being there, and shortly afterwards Jack brought her up to the room. He said he hoped she wouldn't mind us playing a child's board game. It was an old custom of ours, he said.

THE MERCHANT, THE KING AND THE QUEEN

It was all right by her, she said, and I could see that she enjoyed it, watching us two brothers. And she became interested in the game, too, in its complexity and in the shades of its meaning and purpose. I played recklessly, ignoring the warriors and the fortresses. I lost pieces and failed to store tokens. Jack, meanwhile, played very carefully and solidly, occupying two fortresses and collecting a good number of the amber tokens. I was clearly losing but I felt happy and carefree, certain that, after all, it was just a game and confident that Jack didn't suspect me of playing to lose.

Then the Christ card fell to me. The King was also turned up in front of me. In front of Jack lay the Queen."

At this point in the narrative there was a scribbled note in the margin – also in my father's handwriting. It read as follows: "This card has since been lost and not replaced. ix.ix.55" There was an asterisk over the word Queen.

All at once the fortunes of the game were reversed. The Merchant was mine, and he began winning, however casually I played him. The passes all seemed open to me. Jack lost his fortresses and found himself back at Home. In the end I had to play the Christ card in the Fourth Kingdom and shortly afterwards the Merchant won the Queen. Abruptly, Jack got up and left the room, without a word. The rain had stopped and we heard the outside door below us slam shut. From the window we saw Jack striding over the lawn towards park. Crossing the stile he too slipped and fell heavily in the mud. He got up, cursing, and disappeared out of sight.

Sue was sad for him. "He's just a boy," she said. "It was only a game."

I did not want to fall in love with Sue. But from the beginning it was too late. From the very first moment it was too late.

Jack and I have not played the game since, and only with difficulty have the scars healed between us. I honestly argued with Sue that Jack was a better man than I, but she said, "Better, yes. A man—not yet," and it's possible that in choosing me she was attracted by the big city and the colourful world of commerce. But, knowing her, I think not. Later she began to yearn for the farms and the hedgerows and the sounds of the animals and the clear country phases of the moon.

The instructions to the game appended below are as I remember having them from my father, influenced, no doubt, by what I myself have learned of the play."

The letter was signed William Yeoman, London, 1939

On the next sheet was a list of rules in a small and careful hand; then, at the very end, a scribble in my mother's writing: "I do not love this game. William still won't throw it away, so I am hiding it for another to find. Let him remember that it is just a game. Just a game."

This was signed Susan Yeoman, October 1955."

CHAPTER THREE

THE FRIENDLY HANGMAN

I was fascinated by the game and intrigued by my father's story. My problem now was to find someone to play with. The instructions were that the players must be 'within the family'. My brother was too young—so that left only cousins. I could think of a couple of cousins but they lived some way away and I hardly knew them. There seemed only one possibility: John Hadley. Now Hadley was a second cousin, to be exact he was grandson of my father's uncle. But I thought that he could, at a stretch, be described as 'family'. Besides, there was no one else. It was Hadley or no one.

Hadley and I were at school together, a private prep school situated among the woodlands of central Surrey. He was a bookworm, a fantastic storyteller, a riddler, a chess player, a dictionary of unlikely words, an archive of astonishing histories. We were good friends, Hadley and I, and I knew he would take to the game.

I told him about it on the first evening of term, in September 1960. He wanted to see the game immediately so we headed for the woods as soon as we got the chance. There I unveiled the game and, after insisting on the need for secrecy, started to tell him the first rules. I had already detached my father's letter from the instructions, but Hadley was more interested in the game itself. He rapidly examined the cards and pieces and darted questions at me as to the sequence of play. As soon as he'd understood the basics, he wanted to start a game, but we only had twenty minutes between bells, and anyway I was against it. I wanted to take the first game slowly, and I told him it was unlucky to start a game and not complete it.

"If that's so, we'll never be able to play," Hadley said. "Come on, let's just try a few moves."

At that moment I caught sight of Tom, lurking among the rhododendrons.

"Oh Christ, it's Tom," I said.

"Go away, Tom," Hadley said, crossly.

But Tom wasn't going anywhere, having heard every detail of our conversation. He had already been in the woods when we arrived, he told us, checking out a likely camp for the term.

"And then you two twits turn up," he said, lighting a cigarette.

There were only certain times when we were allowed in the woods, but Charlie Tom ignored this rule. If he was not to be found in the woods, then he was to be found on the edge of the woods, which meant he would soon be in them. Geddes, Hopper and the other masters despaired of controlling him. Regularly he would exceed their limits and be reported to Tyson. Double minuses were issued and even the unprecedented treble.

Tom carried cigarettes and knives, he was wild and tough, a Tom

THE FRIENDLY HANGMAN

Sawyer of suburban Surrey, impervious to beatings and canings, unimpressed by rewards and punishments, instinctively seeking the freedom of the woods. In spite of the grey cotton shirt, the striped tie and the short-trousered suit of his school uniform, he could not be severed from some long tradition of Slav or Romany tribalism. He had thick black hair, dusky face, fingers forever anointed with mud or ink or the dust from the darkest corners of rooms or pockets. He was sick in prayers. He coughed in assemblies even after the most impressive ban. Ink found its way into his white Sunday shirt before church as if magically attracted. He was bottom of the form, last in chits, and generally regarded as something to be hidden away during the visits of parents or prospective parents as they toured the spacious grounds. His essay on Magellan's voyage around the world remains in my mind as a masterpiece of economy. "It was ruff," was all he had to say.

Tom gave me a cigarette. It was he who had taught me to smoke when we were eight, in the garden of his home among the great sandy pines of Oxshott Woods. He had in his possession some stale, grubby Weights that made me feel sick and excited. His camp at home was a primitive yurt, circular and perfectly concealed, and it was just such a camp that he made made each term in the school woods. In fact, that first day of term he had already chosen his spot and started to build. His suit was filthy.

"You'll catch it for that," I said.

I often worried on his account, but he never worried on his own.

"It's nothing," he said, and brushed off a couple of pine needles. "Come and see the camp I'm making."

Hadley was still trying to get rid of him.

"Go away, dirty Tom," he said. Tom's presence upset him. They were chalk and cheese.

Tom ignored him and turned to me. "Look, Yeoman, if you let me in on your game, you can use my camp. You'll need somewhere safe, and I'll be around to protect your secrets."

"The game's only for us," said Hadley shortly.

"Oh, I don't want to play," said Tom. "I'll watch."

The camp was superbly sited. Even Hadley saw that. A round bowl lined with pine needles with a rampart running in a circle among the thick rhododendron bushes, it was cosy and secluded. For a reason that I did not then understand, I was keen for Tom to be a witness to the game. Perhaps I was afraid that Hadley and I were too alike, and not well suited to the occult world of shaded woods and furtive deeds, which was Tom's natural element.

The bell clanged dully and we ran back to the new term of bells and more bells, ticks and pluses, tuckshop and grace and that smell — that infernal smell which drifted from the big kitchens, steaming out at first in warm billows of cabbage and gravy, curling around the door to the staff room, where it picked up a cloud of tobacco and chair-leather and book-dust; then through the immaculate library, with its thick carpet and tall shelves, to the corridor outside Tyson's study, where it collected traces of polish and mop water; on past the washrooms and urinals, getting an injection of a fourth set of whiffs and to the bootroom, a little sanctuary of leather and dubbin and dry mud; through the changing rooms and showers; past the games board and at last into the gym, the setting of Tyson's most famous performances.

He was king of the heap, cock of the walk, a very popinjay in his silk-lined master's gown, his broad, bright club ties, his glasses and his ominous shoes. He was particularly bad that term. He was suffering from ulcers and he was very angry. I think that anger was his most enduring passion. He was angry at the staff, the boys, the cooks, the cleaners, the weather, the cars, the road system, governments and the billions and billions of *idiots* who make up the entire population of this planet, if one left aside two or three select men like himself, certain friends of his, and Winston Churchill.

He hated Tom, of course, with a deep loathing. Hadley he largely ignored. Hadley could hardly find real favour in his eyes and he in turn must have suspected that Hadley's original mind was capable of hatching subversion. Also Hadley was one of those people whose boot always travels further than the ball when he tries to kick a football, and I can remember some truly abysmal scores of his on the shooting range. Such performances gave Tyson an excuse for a fusillade of accurate, penetrating shots of his own. But on the whole Tyson kept clear of Hadley, not even bothering to make a target of Hadley's perpetually runny nose.

That term began with the caning of four boys who had

happened to run through the warm ashes of some fire extinguished the day before. The woods were put out of bounds for a week. We tried playing the game under the bushes by the monkey puzzle tree, but there was continual traffic of boys and we gave up.

Then Harkus lost his football jersey, and the whole school was ransacked to look for it. That week's film was cancelled, and the woods stayed out of bounds.

Then Garrick and I dropped the S.S.Britannia, a toy boat, outside the rifle range, and on the same day a scratch was discovered on the inside leg of the grand piano. These momentous events occasioned an almost apoplectic outburst of Tyson's fury. He had the cess pits cleaned out and the woods were still out of bounds.

Finally, Tom insisted that we go anyway and play the opening game, whatever the ruling on the woods. Personally, he said, it hadn't made any difference to his own movements whether the woods were out of bounds or not.

In fact it proved easy enough to slip into the woods one free afternoon and finally the game was set out. It took us a while to grasp its rudiments. We only got as far as the Second Kingdom. For most of the game we were involved in a long struggle for possession of the Rings. I drew the Friendly Hangman early on in the game and it shocked me anew to see Tyson's eyes staring out at me from my hand.

The Hangman in the First Kingdom is a powerful figure, especially when securely lodged in a fortress. He executed Hadley's first warrior and stopped the passes. Then Hadley drew Pellinore, a card showing an ancient warrior who looked something like Alice's White Knight as Tenniel had imagined him. He was apparently the least powerful of the three warriors, but he had an extraordinary resilience: you could defeat him again and again in battles but he kept coming back. Hadley was most impressed by him; he was exactly the sort of hero he admired, melancholy and unimposing yet stubborn and hardy and protected by some sort of ancient innocence. The Hangman lured him into the citadel and put him on trial, but Pellinore defeated the Judge and escaped.

The Hangman finally won that first game for me, but it was curious how far my sympathies were with Pellinore, and I was glad at the end when he managed to return to the freedom of the forest.

Those first games were unexciting compared to our later struggles. It took us time to learn the pieces and strategies. More often than not the game resolved itself into a struggle for the Rings, and often these two characters, Pellinore and the Hangman, were the chief protagonists. Hadley discarded the Hangman the few times that he drew him, announcing that he had conceived a dislike for that particular card, but he went out of his way to get Pellinore.

I had almost forgotten the mysterious potential of the game, of which my father's letter had warned me, but I was intrigued by these confrontations between Pellinore and the Hangman. You could hardly imagine more different characters. The Hangman was all subterfuge and conspiracy. He was a faithful servant of the King, and whenever the King was turned up to me the pair became virtually unassailable in the First Kingdom. But Pellinore appeared to have the gift of attracting the loyalty of other characters within the citadel itself. The Merchant, the Priest and even the Judge were drawn in this way and Hadley pointed out to me that he could see nothing in the rules to account for this curious magnetism. It was as if, he said, it could be explained in terms of Pellinore's character alone.

"He's like all of those old, rather hopeless warriors engaged on an endless quest," he said. "He has neither youth nor great strength nor magical weaponry. He could never stand against Lancelot or Beowulf or Achilles, and yet he endures. Nothing can shake his resolve. And he has the power of loneliness as well. He has no servants or companions. He's all by himself. But what I want to know is this: how does the game make it possible for him to emerge like this? I mean it's only cards and dice and a board, isn't it?"

I said nothing.

"Well, isn't it?" he insisted.

I had told him nothing of my father's letter or of Em Sharp's warning. I felt a little jealous of the game and its associations. It really belonged to my family after all. Perhaps I thought that any mysteries deriving from the game should properly concern me and me alone.

"Of course it is," I answered him.

"Then what's all this secrecy for? Why do we have to play it down in the woods with the infernal Tom watching? Incidentally, some tokens have disappeared."

I took them out and counted them. He was right. About half a dozen of the amber coloured beads were missing.

"Tom took them," Hadley said emphatically.

"Of course he didn't," I said. "What would Tom want with a few beads? We must have dropped them at the camp."

"Well, maybe. But I should keep an eye on them from now on. They are amber, aren't they?"

"Surely not."

"I bet they are. That's why Tom took them. But look, if there's no mystery to this game, then why don't we play it openly? Why don't we play it with some of the others?"

"I told you it has to stay in the family. Sort of family tradition, I suppose. It was one of the instructions, remember?"

"I think there's something you're not telling me. You may as well because I'll find out anyway, you know."

"I don't know any more than you do."

Tyson's ulcers had been getting worse. He was close to driving himself and everyone else round the bend. His latest campaign was the most ludicrous of all. Now, twenty-five years later, I cannot believe that anyone present at the time can have forgotten the episode of the dirty pants.

One morning Tyson kept the boys in the gym after morning prayers. The staff, apart from Miss Daphne, the school matron, were allowed to leave – to their great relief, no doubt. A large cardboard box was produced and placed ceremoniously on Tyson's table.

Tyson stood behind the small table desk and took off his thick-lensed glasses and rubbed them carefully with the hem of his gown, "When it comes to the point," he said, "that this school must be disgraced in the eyes of the good traders and merchants of the neighbouring town, and when everybody behind the scenes here has to put up with what I can only call shameful personal dirtiness, then I am prepared to come down very heavily on those boys responsible. Miss Daphne will tell you," here he half-turned to the auburn-haired Miss Daphne, who stood behind him looking unusually irritated, "that the number of dirty pants going off to the laundry each week has increased to the point of embarrassment and shame. I have here, in this box, the dirtiest."

I can hardly convey the degree of concealed fury with which Tyson spoke these words – spoke all of his words when launching one of his public attacks – nor how effectively he reminded his audience of his absolute mastery of their fortunes.

He opened the box.

"Here are…," For a moment we thought he was actually going to display the offending articles. "Here are the names of the worst cases." He looked at a paper lying on the desk and read out twelve names, slowly, some of them with more distaste than others. Then he wandered down the aisle between the rows of benches, casting his searching gaze among the boys, catching the guilty glances.

"You…And you…And you, Johnny Garrick, should know better.

A dormitory captain, a first eleven footballer…Of course some boys do have problems of sweat. You, Johnny Garrick, run about all the time, putting a lot of effort into your games. Come here, Garrick." He returned to the desk and sat down. "Come here Johnny Garrick." And Garrick came out from the back bench of the choir, blushing and grinning sheepishly, to stand by the desk where Tyson put his arm out and caught him round the waist and gave him an appraising look. "Strapping great lad you are, Garrick. How much do you weigh?"

"Ten stone." Garrick was beginning to relax before this familiar kind of praise.

"Ten stone. And how tall are you?"

"Five eight."

"Five foot eight inches and ten stone and only twelve years old. And how many goals have you scored this term, Garrick?"

"Fourteen, sir." Garrick swayed on his heels a little, bashfully.

"Well, I'll give you fourteen of the best if you send in dirty pants to the laundry again," said Tyson, rising and catching John Garrick by the neck and push-pull-pushing him back to his place. But the light relief, the little apologetic gesture to the heroes of bat and ball, was over, and turning back into the aisle Tyson addressed the school in a quiet and menacing tone. "Pants will be inspected next week and if there are any dirty pants in Monday's laundry, let me tell you, there'll be hell to pay."

Tom, who was sitting next to me, whispered something in my ear that I failed to catch.

But Tyson pounced.

THE FRIENDLY HANGMAN

"Ah. Tom has something to say. Silence, boys, while we listen to what the wise Tom has to add to my remarks. Go on, Tom. We weren't fortunate enough to hear what you were saying."

The silence was complete.

"We're waiting, Tom."

"Nothing, sir."

"What do you mean, nothing, you leant over to Yeoman, your lips moved but you said *nothing*?"

Another silence.

"If you have difficulty remembering, Tom, you can come with me to my study now and I'll see if I can help to jog your memory," Tyson was leaning over our bench and his face seemed colossal, all his anger bunched in his forehead. There was a little line of sweat over the bridge of his nose.

Tom cleared his throat. "I said I couldn't see the point of sending clean pants to the laundry, sir," he announced, very quietly.

Not many of us heard him, but Tyson did. He looked like a venomous snake that someone had dared to slap in the face.

"I'll deal with you later, Tom," he hissed, "I swear I will." Then, to the rest of the school, "The learned Tom thinks I have been joking. He will find out that I have not. And in case any of the rest of you should be tempted to agree with him, let me add that I shall be making certain impromptu inspections of my own, and woe betide those who have chosen to ignore this warning."

With that he gathered up the folds of his gown and swept from the room.

THE FRIENDLY HANGMAN

Tom arrived in the dormitory that night after what had obviously been an extremely painful interview with his Headmaster. He went to his bed and began undressing in silence. I knew then how much it must have hurt him, because every time he'd been caned before he'd had something cheerful and impertinent to say.

But we persuaded him to let us see his honourable wounds – his war wounds, so to speak. I was horrified. There must have been a dozen livid welts across his backside. One or two of the strokes had drawn blood. None of us had seen anything like it.

The Friendly Hangman. It was true, in a way. He was friendly to me, after his fashion with favourites. And I was often his disciple. That was the trouble. Tyson was a violent and frequently terrifying man, but also I believed that he was, in the main, right. He had to be right. He was 'in loco parentis', in the place of the parent, as he never tired of reminding us. He had the blessing of my parents. When they had turned me over to his charge at the age of seven I had accepted unquestioningly that the authority that had been my father's was now his. I was a trusting and loyal little fellow, eager to behave well, to do what was expected of me. Tyson himself was clearly respected and applauded by all the parents and by a great proportion of the staff, and at the age of seven there was nothing in my instinct to tell me to keep clear of him, quite unlike Tom or Hadley, or even John Garrick who shrugged his broad shoulders and slept the sleep of the just.

THE FRIENDLY HANGMAN

The games with Hadley began to change in character. With our growing understanding of the pieces and their functions, we moved more often into the Third and Fourth Kingdoms. Hadley, especially, began turning away from the fortresses and setting his sights towards the centre of the board. Often he overstretched himself and got cut off in impossible situations, but he seemed to give little importance to winning, which he apparently regarded as a mere technicality. He concentrated only on his progress towards the centre, and many times I beat him from the Second or Third Kingdom when he was already in the Fourth.

"What happens when you get to the middle, Yeoman," he asked one day during break. We were walking the small triangle hand in hand.

"You win the game, you dope."

"Yes I know, but it can't just be like the other ways of winning the game. I mean yesterday I won from the Second Kingdom. We reached a stalemate and I won on tokens. How can that possibly be the same as reaching the centre, the black hole at the centre? Why did they colour it black?"

I didn't know, but when he explained I agreed with him. The black made the centre seem like a hole in the board, a hole to another dimension. Like a gateway in the hollow earth, an entrance to the underworld.

"So what is supposed to happen when you reach the centre, Yeoman?"

I, too, had thought of this, in my own way. My father's letter had not mentioned reaching the centre and I felt sure that if it had happened in his experience, he would have referred to it. Abruptly I decided to give Hadley my father's letter to read.

He read it through as soon as I handed it to him. We were in the corner of the sixth form. His desk was the first in the class, as usual. He frowned as he read, and once or twice he sighed. At the end he blew his nose repeatedly.

"You should have shown me this before." He looked back at the letter, and re-read something. "So the girl is your Mum."

"Yes."

"What's your uncle like?"

I told him.

"Have you ever thought that your uncle would make a better Dad than your father?"

I laughed, embarrassed at the thought.

Hadley spoke in a whisper, even though there was no one else in the room. "Look, Yeoman, you should have told me this before because we may have wasted time, or, worse still, we may have already been influencing events in our games without understanding what we were doing." He placed an odd emphasis on these last words. "I don't think your father understood either, but probably your uncle Jack did."

I got out the character cards and found the Friendly Hangman.

"Look at it carefully," I said. "Look at the eyes behind the glasses. Can't you see who it is?"

And all at once he could. "It's Tyson," he murmured. "How come

I never saw that before?" He studied the face again. "How long have you known this?" he asked me.

"It was the first thing I saw," I told him.

"But why didn't you tell me?"

I didn't answer him. I was thinking of something else. It was suddenly clear to me that, if Tyson was the Friendly Hangman, then Avery was Pellinore. Fred Avery was Assistant Headmaster. He was a rough, gravelly man who looked older than he was. He didn't smile much and his brusque manner made him an object of fear to some of the boys, especially the younger ones. But if you liked Latin, or football, you got to like him, too. He didn't bother to hide his contempt for Tyson. During Tyson's more extravagant outbursts at mealtimes, he could be seen muttering oaths under his breath. Now, if Avery was Pellinore…

The bell for tea clanged loudly from the corridor. The school assembled in the gym and fell into its usual ranks. Eagles led off, then Hawks, then Swifts, then Owls. Hadley and I were both Swifts. Tom was an Eagle, but not one of the four sections really wanted him.

I didn't tell Hadley of my idea until we were well into the next game. The woods were once more in bounds and Tom was absent, organising battles. The Hangman was again in possession of the Rings. Hadley was excited by the new possibilities of the game, and especially by the thought that the Hangman was Tyson.

"If only we could think of a way to get him," he said.

THE FRIENDLY HANGMAN

Pellinore was again in his hand. He was in the Forests of the Second Kingdom, preparing to broach the pass into the Third.

"Let's have a dekko at the Pellinore card, Hadley," I said.

He passed it over and I looked at it carefully. I was after a sign, a confirmation of my idea. It had been there all the time, but only now did I see it. In his right hand Pellinore held a sword. The ring and little fingers of this hand, instead of helping to grip the sword, were bunched uncomfortably behind it. The hand had been represented in such a way as to to draw attention to this feature.

The fourth and fifth fingers of Avery's right hand also refused to open, and at all times remained folded against his palm.

I threw the card triumphantly down on the board. "Look at his fingers, Hadley," I cried.

When he'd seen what I'd seen he understood immediately. We all knew about Avery's fingers. It was quite a shock when you first shook hands with him.

"So Fred is Pellinore," said Hadley. His eyes were shining. "Now we know what to do."

"What?"

"Let him defeat the Hangman, of course."

At first I objected. I felt unwilling to surrender my own position. I even felt slightly protective of Tyson. I thought we ought to be careful of what we did to him. But Hadley pointed out emphatically that Tyson was a dangerous man, becoming more dangerous, and that Fred was a far superior character. He began to list for me some of the episodes of the term. He also told me that I was stupid not to realise that if the Hangman was real, and Pellinore was real, then some or all of the other characters were real too, and that as long as I went on treating them as mere cards I was wasting them, or worse.

"Anyway, you don't play the game well," he complained.

"What do you mean? I *win*, don't I?"

"Yes, you win, technically, but you don't progress. The way you play just serves to prevent me from progressing. As long as I play with you," he continued moodily, "I haven't got a chance of getting to the Fifth Kingdom. You just go for the citizens and the warriors, and settle in somewhere to amass beads. Don't you understand that the guides are the important characters and that the true interest of the game starts in the Third Kingdom? You must learn to follow the guides, Yeoman."

We played on, but instead of progressing to the Third Kingdom, Pellinore returned to the Rings and launched an attack on the Hangman. The King was turned up to Hadley and the Judge defected to Pellinore. The Hangman was left alone in his citadel where he was stripped of his tokens, one by one. Finally he was defeated and out of the game. Hadley was allowed one further, courtesy throw. He threw a six, which took him to the toll-gate, and from there he travelled directly to the Ramparts where he threw another six and a four. This brought him to Barrow Hill where he threw the red dice and entered the Third Kingdom. There, at the Healing Stone, he made contact with Christ.

CHAPTER FOUR

PELLINORE AND PUCK

THE news soon broke that Tyson had been ordered a complete rest. He retired to his bedroom upstairs where his housekeeper, waited on him. Avery took temporary charge. The school breathed a sigh of relief and Hadley was delighted. We were both certain that the game was beginning to work.

We had agreed not to tell Tom of the new developments. Anyway he had been greatly offended when we had accused him of stealing the beads.

"Beads?" he said contemptuously. "What would I want with *beads*?"

And he made himself scarce for a while.

Tyson got no better and, to everyone's delight, it was announced by Fred Avery that the headmaster was to withdraw to the seaside for a week or so, and that he himself would be acting in his place for the time being.

It was early October. There was a spell of mild, fine weather, and an almost complete respite from the more disagreeable aspects of school life. Bells rang less urgently. Mistakes and minor infringements went unreported and unpenalised. Mr. Hopper scored the first recorded 50 on the shooting range, and was so embarrassed at his own achievement that he walked around watching the floor for a weekend. Hadley and I left our game where it was. I played football endlessly and Hadley resumed his friendship with poor Abbott who had been too shy and polite to complain of how he'd been neglected.

Tyson's convalescence was extended to two weeks. The first rehearsals of the school play took place without him, and the actors were spared his rantings and his tireless tyranny. A report went round that Fred had been seen talking with Geddes one night in Tyson's study and a plot against Tyson was rumoured.

In this blessed pause, Fred seemed indeed like the White Knight. He performed all his public functions with the minimum of fuss. While he never obviously disregarded any of the mass of rules and regulations that ordered all our lives, he was not inclined to treat them as of any more than superficial importance. We had always known that Tyson's manias were a bane to him, but he had remained somewhat in the shadows except where his beloved football and his beloved dead languages were concerned. Now we saw him clearly for the first time: what had seemed clumsy in him now seemed subtle and what had seemed brusque now seemed deft.

One afternoon there was a big match and a lot of parents came to watch. The school team won. Afterwards there was one of those standing tea-parties that visiting parents seemed to like so much. Outside, dusk had fallen and it had suddenly grown cold, and there was a great fire in the library. As a member of the team I was present to make polite conversation and politely receive congratulations for having scored two goals against Wootton Trinkett. At one point I found myself next to Mr. Avery. He smiled and shook hands and helped a lady to cake, but he could not resist muttering under his breath the sort of comments that the parents were not likely to understand but that told us quite clearly what he thought of these charades and how highly he prized our generous victory.

I watched him, too, shaking hands on the way out and noticed the pair of fingers that refused to to straighten, enabling him to escape the complete gesture of fealty towards these accountants and merchants and lawyers and farmers, whose only quality in his eyes lay in their having a male offspring of an age suitable to be initiated into the secrets of Latin grammar and attacking football.

But then Tyson returned, two days early, full of life and fight. Genial and breezy, he strode into tea on Saturday and announced that he was well again and delighted to be back in this best of all possible schools, among the best of all possible pupils. He picked out a dozen of his favourites, teasing and pinching thighs. He was out to win applause, and as ever I found myself falling under his spell.

Tyson stalked the room, his shoes squelching loudly.

"Whose fathers have the Distinguished Flying Cross?" he suddenly asked.

I put up my hand, and so did one or two others.

"And whose fathers have the Distinguished Service Order?"

PELLINORE AND PUCK

Sam Oats raised his hand. I left mine raised.

He looked over at me.

"I knew that William Yeoman had the D.F.C. and bar, but I didn't know he had the D.S.O."

He didn't, but I wouldn't admit it. To please Tyson and to polish some part of my ego, I awarded my father the D.S.O.

Tyson often spoke of the war. He worshipped not only Churchill but also Montgomery, Alexander, Mountbatten and Eisenhower. He hated Hitler, of course, together with all the Nazi leaders, and the Japanese. He had some liking for the Americans but tended to consider them ungentlemanly. The fighter pilots of the Battle of Britain were his especial heroes, while those who manned the small boats at Dunkirk, the desert tank regiments and even the Ghurkas came close to matching them in his regard. The Ghurkas, however, may also have been associated in his mind with the treacherous soldiers of the Indian mutiny, for he could never entirely trust anyone who wasn't a Caucasian – the Jamaican cricketer Learie Constantine being closest to an exception.

The D.F.C. and D.S.O. were eminent awards in Tyson's view. He had not fought in the war but he was fiercely approving of those who had, and would do more than most of them to keep alive the memory of their feats. My father, for example, was genuinely embarrassed to be reminded of his part in the war, I think because he had lost some of his closest friends in it. Like Tyson, I didn't know what war was, but I thought it had to do with glory.

It was Tom, again, who spoilt Tyson's show. During a pause in the the proceedings he retched loudly and then vomited. I was sitting opposite him and had seen him turning green. It may have been the food that had upset him – he was prone to such violent revolutions of the stomach – but it was also, undoubtedly, some deep nausea at Tyson's performance. Tyson was furious, close to apoplexy. His genial mood dissipated instantly, he uttered some words of pure loathing and strode from the room.

Late that evening Tom was summoned from our dormitory to Tyson's study. He returned half an hour later and slipped wordlessly into bed, but I leant over and asked him what had happened.

"He's expelled me," said Tom. "I'm not allowed to come back next term."

The next day the whole school knew of Tom's punishment. Hadley and I talked of it during break.

"It's monstrous," said Hadley. He was not fond of Tom himself, but he was moved to eloquence by his sense of the injustice. "The only reason Tyson's getting rid of Tom is because he doesn't fit into his narrow idea of what people ought to be like. I expect we'll hear next that Tom is to be 'moved on because he needs more help with his academic work' or something like that, when we all know it's really because he was sick at supper. But who will ever dare say so?"

"Pellinore?" I ventured. We had taken to referring to Avery by his Arthurian name.

"No, he doesn't like Tom either. None of them do. They'll all be pleased to see the back of him. What I was wondering was whether we could help him in the game somehow."

"How could we do that?"

"Well, I'm not sure. Perhaps there's a card we could identify him with."

"But we can't do it that way round. I mean, surely we can't make the game do just what we like."

"You could be right. But if we looked through the cards we might find one to help us. Let's try it anyhow."

We did try it, although I felt rather hopeless about the whole thing. Tom seemed such an unlikely character to identify among the figures of *Albion's Dream*.

We looked through all the cards anyway, setting on one side those cards which we thought bore any conceivable resemblance to the Tom that we knew. At the end there were only three: the Soldier, the Priest, and one of the guides, Puck. The soldier was small and dark, a bit like Tom, and the Priest, said Hadley, had a slightly furtive expression that reminded him of Tom when he was up to no good. But the one I favoured was Puck. He was small and elusive and had a mischievous look.

"The trouble is," Hadley said, "that Puck is a guide and therefore an important character in the Inner Kingdoms. Tom is just an unlucky rogue. It doesn't fit."

But while he was speaking I was studying the Puck card again.

In the background was a circle of trees, clearly meant as Puck's dwelling.

"He lives in the woods," I said. "That's a good sign."

Hadley took the card and looked at it minutely.

"Yeoman, look among the trees. Can you see it?"

Faint, but distinct when you spotted it, was the outline of an earthen rampart, half hidden among the circle of pines. It was just such a camp as Tom had made in the woods a hundred times.

That settled it. Tom became Puck.

Tyson had expelled Tom, but that was not enough. He seemed unable to leave him alone. He picked on him endlessly, making him the butt of his bitter sarcasms, holding him up to ridicule at every opportunity. For his part, Tom seemed to have lost the will to fight. His face had changed from its normal healthy brown to the colour of ash. He wandered about the school like a sad ghost, hanging his head and refusing all attempts to cheer him up.

"Come on, Tom," I said to him. "It's not as bad as all that. Perhaps your next school will be better. Perhaps you'll like it."

"Perhaps."

"Anyway, it's only a few weeks more."

"Yes."

"Let's go and have a smoke."

"No thanks."

With a sure instinct for what would hurt Tom most, Tyson had confined him to the school buildings. Such restrictions had never made any difference to Tom before, but this time he meekly obeyed. He seemed to have accepted Tyson's judgement of him – he was no good, a no-hoper. At the age of twelve he had been declared a pariah and he had resigned himself to it.

For a while Hadley and I couldn't help Puck in our games. We had agreed that what we had to do was to engineer a confrontation between Puck and the Hangman, but not in the First Kingdom, where the Hangman was strong. We had to be sure that the odds were stacked in Puck's favour.

Then one day I drew Puck in what seemed an ideal situation. I already had Pellinore and Thor in the Second Kingdom. Hadley was at the Rings with the Hangman and the King. When he got through the Toll-Gate and entered the Second Kingdom, he installed himself at Barrow Hill. There I attacked him with my warriors, but the Hangman threw faultlessly and managed to command the loyalties first of Thor and then of Pellinore. Puck was left on his own, and although for a while he evaded his enemies, they hunted him down and surrounded him. He was probably finished anyway at this point, but he threw so badly that the King didn't even have to use his warriors, and Puck, too, was enlisted in his service. It was the first time we had seen a guide commanded by the King.

I was left with no pieces and so the game was over. We dreaded to think what effect our play might have on Puck's fortunes, although I could hardly imagine what could be worse than the sentence of expulsion and Tom's dismal acquiescence.

But things did get worse. Seeing how Tom was cowed, Tyson began to change his tactics. Instead of bullying him, he appeared to befriend him – or not exactly to befriend him, but to use him. One morning there were some exercise books to be distributed at assembly.

"Come here Tom and hand them out," Tyson said.

The whole school watched while Tom came obediently to the table, collected the books and handed them out. Then he returned to the table.

"Will that be all, sir?"

"Yes. Thank you Tom," and Tyson patted his head, as a man might pat the head of his faithful dog.

Tom even began to encourage these attentions. "Can I help you with that, sir?" "Is there anything I can do, sir?"

It hurt me deeply seeing Tom in this role. All his natural mischief was gone, and with it everything that we had always known him for. We were used to him as the bad boy, the troublemaker, the villain of the piece, and never had we been so aware of the debt we all owed to him, how he had borne all the sharpest of Tyson's attacks.

I wished we had never tried to help him with the game.

"I don't think we should play again," I told Hadley. "Or if we do we should remove the Puck card from the pack."

Hadley was surprisingly angry at this suggestion.

"That's your trouble," he said. "You never really accepted that it's more than a game. So now, when it suits you, you just think 'I won't play any more'. You want to put it away like a toy you've grown out of. But you can't do that Yeoman. We're in it up to the neck."

He was so slightly built, Hadley, always so pale and nervous looking, so remote from the world of action – at least the world of action as we experienced it – that it seemed odd, the power of his seriousness. I now think that if it had not been for him, with his commitment to what he saw as the peculiar workings of the game, that I would have pulled out at this point. But I deferred to him and we played on.

It was mid-November and the playing of the game out of doors was becoming more and more uncomfortable. If Tom had been around he would have improved the amenities of the camp; as it was we were often cold and damp. But we couldn't think of anywhere else to play where we would be safe from interruption, and perhaps it reassured us to think that we were playing in Puck's favourite place.

In the next game I drew him early on. I ignored the First Kingdom and concentrated on getting hold of the warriors. Luck was with me and Puck reached the Dungeon where he was joined by Pellinore, Galahad and Thor, and they proceeded together to the Third Kingdom. At this point I drew Death and had to throw the red dice. It was five to one against throwing Doom, but that is what I did. I dared not look at Hadley. I felt as if I had done it on purpose, as if it were my fault that Tom's life, as I saw it, was being put at risk.

I now had to throw the white dice to see how many of my players were to die. A four or more would kill Puck. I threw a three.

I surrendered my warriors cheerfully, and on the very next turn I drew Merlin. A mage with a guide in the Third Kingdom is in an extremely strong position, so, from despairing at Puck's imminent death, I suddenly found myself at large in the Kingdom of stone. It was one of the qualities of the game, the way fortunes could be reversed in a moment.

In this instance, Death had removed three warriors from my hand, but at a time when their power was already waning. The zenith of the warriors' might is in the Second Kingdom, the age of Bronze. Still powerful in the Stone Age, by the time of the Drift they are inferior to both mages and guides, which meant that Death's triple harvest had little effect on my position, especially since I had drawn Merlin. Then Hadley drew the Christ card. Like my uncle Jack, Hadley had a great liking for this card although as yet it had brought him little luck. So it proved again. A long struggle followed at the Healing Stone, between Merlin and Puck on the one hand, and Christ and Hod on the other, Merlin finally producing a spell which bound his opponents to the spot. Puck then led him to the Fourth Kingdom, and with Hadley incrennellated, I had a succession of throws to win control of the winds and find the entrance to the mysterious Fifth Kingdom. I think I preferred to fail. Anyway, it took an extraordinary combination of cards and dice to arrive at the entrance, the elusive Caer Sidh, and truly I lacked the resolve. Something about the Black Ring and the Giant's Grave filled me with fear, as if I would find a rip in the fabric of things and fall through it.

When I failed, Hadley accused me of not trying. He was very acute in some ways, John Hadley.

I acquitted myself by reminding him of what I had done for Puck. I had left him, unscathed and victorious, deep within the Fourth Kingdom.

"If that three had been a four!…" Hadley said solemnly.

When we got back to the school, I looked around for Tom, but he was nowhere to be found.

"He's gone away," Garrick told me. "Somebody came and fetched him in a car."

"Who? Why?"

"I don't know. His Dad, perhaps."

I'd never met his father. He seemed to be always away from home, a member of the armed forces or something. But it sounded like good news: at least Tom was out of the Hangman's clutches.

We didn't notice that Fred Avery was not in his customary place the following lunchtime, and even the subsequent rumour that he was ill did not strike us as ominous. The weekend followed, football was cancelled by an incessant driving rain, and so Fred was not much missed. On Monday morning Tom reappeared.

I saw immediately that he was back to normal. The proper twinkling mischief was in his eye.

"What happened Tom? Where have you been?"

It had been his Dad who had come for him. He had been abroad and had just got back when he heard about his son's expulsion.

"I thought he'd be furious, you see. But he wasn't. He was great!"

Tom was very happy, remembering it. "He told me I shouldn't worry about it at all, that he'd never trusted Tyson anyway, and that we'd go and find a much better school, with a decent headmaster. I never realised Dad felt like that. He even told me that I could stay at home, not come back at all. But I came. I want to stay for a while – long enough to get even with Tyson. I've got a plan, you see."

Whereupon he suggested a stroll to the monkey puzzle tree. There he produced some Weights and offered me one. I had known him to smoke in the woods often enough, but the monkey puzzle was a mere twenty yards from one of the dormitories and close to a busy footpath. Tom clearly felt past caring. I was so happy to see him well and wicked again that I took the cigarette and lit up, although I trod it out a few puffs later, as soon as I heard someone coming up the path. Tom smoked on nonchalantly.

His plan was devastatingly simple. He was going to make a mantrap in the woods, lure Tyson there one evening and – Wham! there he'd be, stuck in the trap. With any luck he'd be there all night, and perhaps most of the next day. By this time Tom would have packed his belongings and departed, *in a taxi*. This was the crowning part of the plan.

What sort of a trap did he have in mind, I asked him.

"Well, I'll need a bit of help to dig it, of course, but it'll have to be deep enough so he can't get out. Then I thought of some stakes set in the ground at the bottom. I've got a wizard knife for sharpening them …"

PELLINORE AND PUCK

And he took it out to show me.

The same day the rumour of Fred Avery's illness was confirmed. With what seemed to us undue haste, a replacement had been appointed and was shortly due to arrive.

Hadley came looking for me during break. I saw him coming and tried to avoid him. His solemnity was beginning to unnerve me. He came up beside me and caught my sleeve.

"Leave off a bit, Hadley," I said. "Let's give it a break for a while, shall we?"

You see, Tom was well again, and I'd been badly scared by what hung on the throw of the dice.

"We can't," Hadley said in an urgent undertone.

Reluctantly, I drew away from the group to hear him.

"Fred's ill."

"So what?" I must have been very stupid.

"Pellinore's ill. Don't you see? Ill enough for them to find someone else to teach Latin. He's only been away three days and already they've found a replacement. That means they must have started looking the first day he was away. What does that mean Yeoman?"

The horror of what I had done rushed in on me all at once. In the excitement of saving Puck, I had forgotten completely about Pellinore. I had given Pellinore up to Death in order to save Puck without even a thought of what might happen to Avery. Knowing that, even if I had, I could hardly have played otherwise, didn't help. The essence of the horror, as perhaps of all horror, was a feeling of being utterly alone. I caught hold of Hadley – he whom two minutes ago I had been trying to shrug off – to confirm his complicity, his share in the blame. He was too good and too brave a person to deny it, and yet it made no real difference. I felt as a murderer must feel when the police clap handcuffs on him. I had to sit down. Hadley sat beside me.

"How badly is he ill, Hadley?"

"I don't know. But it must be pretty bad."

"He's not going to die, is he?" Hadley said nothing. "Hadley, he's not, is he?"

"We have to play again, Edward. It's the only way."

"No, I won't play. I won't ever play again. I'll burn the thing. I don't want to see it again."

"Yes, I know how you feel, but if we don't play again, and he *does* die, what then? Shouldn't we have a go, anyway?"

At first I stuck to my refusal, but I was truly afraid of throwing the dice again, of seeing Pellinore show up among my cards, of having his life in my hands. It seemed easier to close my mind to the whole thing. I found myself looking back with extraordinary nostalgia at the time before I had discovered the game. Since the moment I had moved the bookshelf, three months before, I had lived more or less under the shadow of *Albion's Dream*. But Hadley was right: I couldn't make the shadow go away by closing my eyes.

There was a light drizzle falling that afternoon and it was cold. There were no sports, no going outside. Hadley and I had to use the route through the window outside the dormitory called White Cliffs. Everybody else seemed to be having a good time. Abbott, as usual, was curled up in the corner of the sixth form reading a book. Garrick and Austen were lying on the library floor leafing through pages of the guns and tanks of modern warfare. The gym was the scene of a dozen different games. I had our game wrapped in a mackintosh under my arm. Just about everybody wanted to know where we were going. Our furtiveness showed on our faces, I suppose, as is the way when young boys have something to hide. You try as hard as you can to suppress it and yet it shines from you like a beacon.

Hadley especially was a poor conspirator. He told everybody a little too quickly that he was going to practise piano. There was a piano, it's true, in the bow window outside White Cliffs, but his answer failed to explain my presence at his side, failed to explain the bundle under my arm, and signally failed to explain the thick air of plot that lay between us. In the end, even the fellow who was actually practising the piano outside White Cliffs asked us what we were up to. Hadley had had enough. We fled wordlessly through the window.

At the camp the ground was sodden—a condition we soon shared. The wind blew nastily in through a chink in the bushes. More than ever I wished myself back in the time of innocence that summer now represented. How broad and free the trees had been when in full leaf, and how gaunt they had become. We had no sooner started than we were interrupted. I heard footsteps, a twig cracking. Then Hadley heard something. We listened, motionless.

"Must have imagined it," Hadley muttered.

"Must have done," I agreed, not believing it.

We returned to the game, with whatever attention we could muster.

"MUGS," yelled a voice above us.

It was Tom, enjoying a huge joke.

"What a couple of mugs," he said. In the moment that it took me to focus on him, it really was Puck that I saw, a woodland imp, dark as treeshadow and mischievous as the breeze.

Hadley was furious. I was rather relieved. Tom was cheerfully puzzled by our fidelity to our game in such weather.

"Leave the game," he said, "and come and help me start the mantrap." In his hand he carried a garden spade, obviously pinched from the tool sheds. But when he understood that we were set on playing, he was suddenly helpful, gathering brushwood to fill the chinks where the wind blew in and even offering to rig up some kind of shelter.

"If I'd known that you fellows wanted to play in weather like this," he said, "I would have made you a proper job."

"Well never mind now," said Hadley, mollified. "Run along and make your hole."

For I had told him of Tom's plans for Tyson.

"No, I think I'll stay and watch," said Tom. "And look, here's the beads you lost. Found them in the camp." He pulled half a dozen beads from some inner recess. I looked at him sharply, but there was no way of knowing how and when he got hold of them.

PELLINORE AND PUCK

I was pleased to have him stay. He was reassuringly real, reassuringly comfortable in those strange surroundings.

When we started the game again I was praying not to draw Pellinore, but I did. I installed him at the Hermitage, his favourite place. Hadley had Thor, Zoroaster and the Merchant, a formidable trio. With them he entered the Great Maze of Leys. Pellinore was my only player, and the Maze was adjacent to the Hermitage. I threw a one and Pellinore had to enter the Maze. In the Maze, deliberate challenges are impossible, they are produced uniquely by the unpredictable twists and turns of the Maze itself. For me this was the worst possible neck of the woods. I had wanted to hold Pellinore until I was virtually sure of winning. As it was, I stood every chance of losing against Hadley's hand, and yet I couldn't avoid entering the Maze.

I prayed silently that Hadley would quickly find an exit and leave before we met. If I could pick up another warrior or a mage, I would be able to confront him from a strong position.

Instead I drew Puck, a weak character in the Second Kingdom. For a while neither of us could get out of the Maze, and then the worst happened. We met face to face and a challenge was inevitable. Hadley's pieces had a combined value of ten, mine only six. He threw a three, which gave him a total of thirty. I had to throw at least a five.

It was a four. The game was over for me. I looked at Pellinore on the card and thought of his endless and hopeless questing; then I thought of Avery and his subtle kindnesses, the way that his presence in a room stemmed Tyson's worst excesses, of his elegant wife whom we only ever saw from a distance. I was quite certain now that Fred would die and I saw no way of exculpating myself. It seemed that everything that had happened from the discovery of the game to the throw of the four had been leading up to this disaster. Even Hadley, for all his honesty and compassion, would not catch my eye. He had begun to put the game away.

I turned to Tom, whom I had forgotten. He was sitting at a little distance, apparently studying the rules. He looked up.

"What's bothering you two so badly?" he said. "No one would guess you're playing for fun."

This got no answer.

"In fact, I've been wondering about this game of yours. It's some kind of magic, isn't it?"

Again neither of us spoke.

"Well, if it is, I reckon you two are pretty poor magicians. I mean, magic needs some kind of mumbo-jumbo, doesn't it? You sit there shivering with cold, waiting for the dice to tell you the worst—no, my idea of a magician is someone in a fine cloak making his own decisions about who can get away with what. The point of magic is to be powerful, not to wait around until the sky drops on you. Anyway, it seems to me that you two don't even read your own rules properly."

"What do you mean," asked Hadley.

"You were playing in the Maze, weren't you?"

"Yes, why?"

"Well it says in the rules that your guide in the Maze has a special value."

Now he had our interest. I grabbed the rules from where Tom had dropped them. Surely there wasn't anything I could have overlooked. I had seen them dozens of times.

"Where, where?"

"Here. Look." Tom leant over and pointed to some words inserted at the end of the section on the Maze. Somehow I had missed them completely. The instruction was quite clear. 'In the Maze and Troy Town,' it said, 'although within the age of Bronze, the value of the guide is clearly paramount consequently his value is four rather than two'.

Hadley was reading over my shoulder.

"I'd seen that," he said. "How could I have forgotten it?"

So Puck was worth four in the Maze, and Pellinore also four, giving a factor of eight, not six. Eight fours, thirty-two. Pellinore was alive.

Neither Hadley nor I felt like continuing the game, but it hardly seemed necessary anyway. We both felt that Pellinore's miraculous survival was enough to save Fred, and so it proved. That day at tea Tyson came in and made one of his pompous announcements. The Assistant Headmaster, he said, as some of us must have guessed, had been seriously ill and that day had undergone a serious operation. He, Tyson, had seen him immediately after the operation that afternoon, and he was happy to say that it had been successful and that Alfred Avery would certainly make a complete recovery, in time to take up his duties again after Christmas.

Hadley and I did not play *Albion's Dream* again that term.

CHAPTER FIVE

THE BARROW AND THE DOME

THE rest of the term passed in the most gratifyingly normal fashion. The end of the long Michaelmas term is anyway a pleasant time, what with the school play and the Christmas party and the countdown of the days left until Christmas, but mainly I was filled with a blessed relief that I had cast off the burden of the game.

Avery was convalescing; Tom was cheerful. His plan for the mantrap didn't get far, but he clearly disturbed Tyson by his imperviousness to the most extreme form of punishment that had been dealt him. He handed in no work and paid no attention to school routine. In the middle of December, he left – in a taxi, as he had promised. He said a nonchalant goodbye to me, pressing into my hand a packet of Gold Leaf, a broken penknife and some ball bearings. He had mentioned nothing to Tyson about either how or when he would make his departure, slipping out to the local phone box to order the taxi and packing a small suitcase with whatever he considered necessary. The rest of his stuff, including the seventy-five items of the school clothing list, he left where it was.

I missed him, but I couldn't help feeling partly pleased that he had gone. I had always found myself sharing his troubles, but since his illness I had experienced an added feeling of responsibility for him which I did not enjoy. Hadley, on the other hand, seemed genuinely sad. His estimation of Tom changed had completely since he had rescued us that day in the woods and he told me that Tom's words about magic and magicians had shed an entirely new light on the game for him. He was also highly impressed by the way Tom had in reality played the part of the guide in the Maze.

"He became Puck, you see, Yeoman. He was the guide through the Maze. We had got the game wrong and he appeared in the flesh to put us on the right track, and remind us of his true value. I mean, doesn't it strike you as more than odd that Tom, who never reads anything for pleasure, should happen to pick up the instructions and find something that had escaped both of us? And that he should understand the game well enough to appreciate what it was that he had found?"

I had to agree, although I was trying to avoid talking of the game to Hadley then, afraid that he would want to start playing again. I had not seen much of him of late, but I knew that he had been thinking of the game because he told me that he'd been making 'some interesting researches'.

"Now listen to this, for example," he said. "This is Puck from A Midsummer Night's Dream: 'rough, knurly-limbed, faun-faced and shock-pated, a very Shetlander among the gossamer-winged fairies'. Isn't that a perfect description of Tom?"

It was.

THE BARROW AND THE DOME

Then, quite by chance, I made a startling discovery of my own. Tyson had been given a complete set of 1" Ordnance Survey maps. For a few days he was very excited by this addition to his reference library and he had special shelves built to accommodate it. The interest of these maps to boys of our age may seem dubious, but for a while we played at pointing out to one another where we lived, the rivers we fished, the woods we walked in. During one such session, while showing a friend of mine my favourite haunts, I came across Badbury Rings, not many miles from my home in the Blackmoor Vale. The echo of the name in the game struck me immediately and I remembered having once been to Badbury Rings, a series of circular earthworks. The name – 'The Rings' – had always puzzled me, and now I understood what sort of fortress it referred to.

A little later I found Dungeon Hill and then Barrow Hill and, though I could at first hardly believe it, it dawned on me that I had hit upon an actual geography of the game. It was not only the names that corresponded, but the positions they occupied on the board.

I looked for something called the Healing Stone in the appropriate place on the map. At first I could see nothing, then I noticed the village of Shillingstone. At the spot where the Ramparts should have been, was Maiden Castle, which I also remembered having seen from the road, and whose chief feature was a ring of colossal earthen ramparts. Looking for the whereabouts of the maze, I even found, near the village of Leigh, the symbol for an ancient monument and the words Miz-Maz in tiny letters.

I didn't tell Hadley, but I borrowed the OS sheet 178 from the library and made a careful comparison with the names from the game. I couldn't make sense of all of them, but I identified the great majority. It was an exciting thought that I could actually visit some of these places during the holidays. What I expected to find there I'm not quite sure.

Towards the end of term Hadley began pressing me to play once more. He had discovered, he told me, how we could play without being at the mercy of the game's fortunes. He began to tell me, but I cut him short.

"Next term, Hadley. We'll play next term."

We broke up only a week before Christmas. How I loved that magic time between the end of term and the New Year. Of course I enjoyed the Christmas preparations, the decorations, the presents, but what I really loved was some special atmosphere. The fire in the fireplace burnt brighter and smelt sweeter. Whatever the weather did, it seemed right. If it pelted with rain for days and we donned wellingtons and raincoats and caps and tramped off through the muddy fields to give the dogs their daily walk, it seemed fine. If it was clear and icy, it was fine to sit and fish by the river trying to keep your fingertips from freezing, even if it was too cold for the fish to bite. And it was even finer to come home afterwards and kick off your boots and peel off innumerable socks and head for the fireplace and toast crumpets over the fire.

THE BARROW AND THE DOME

I could not decide whether this unique Christmas feeling was generated by the season itself or simply by the sum of everyone's pleasure and goodwill. It was a time of truce. We stopped squabbling in the family, my father gave up his feud with the cat, newspapers were read starting with the sports pages and the crossword and all bans on the watching of T.V. were lifted. Friends called, my elder sister came home for a fortnight, and my father left the little black suitcase up in his bedroom, banishing his work properly for the first time since August.

Three whole months I had been away at school. In that time everything had changed. The leaves were all gone from the elms and the great beeches, the river wore its winter colours, the grass underfoot was coarser and sparser. Best of all, the snipe were back in the field behind the house.

Brandy was overjoyed to see me. His dinners were more generous and his walks longer when I was around, and in the evenings he would come up beside me and sleep with his great head resting on my lap. He was the biggest labrador I've ever seen, I think, half as big again as most labradors and half as beautiful again, too. Technically his colour was yellow, but it deepened to a wonderful golden in the ridge of thick hair along his back, and he had a mane more suitable to a young lion.

He was, without doubt, my best friend, Brandy. We had grown up together (I think he may have been a year or so younger than I) and we knew each other's ways to perfection and neither of us wanted the other to be one whit different, a rare thing even between friends. We walked every day, whatever the weather. Crazy though I was for shooting, I never took the gun when I was with Brandy. He hated guns and would turn tail and flee at the mere sight of one—so when we walked, we just walked, usually over terrain of which we both knew every inch, sometimes further afield.

Christmas passed, and the New Year. My father returned to London. The decorations came down and the house resigned itself to facing the rest of the winter. We were a big family, four children and my parents, and there was a constant coming and going of large numbers of visitors.

And yet I lived a lonely life there, compared to my life at school. Not that it didn't suit me. I never felt the lack of friends. Fishing, shooting, walking—I needed nothing more. Out of doors I had Brandy for company. Indoors I had my mother.

I had no knowledge of farming, of livestock, crops or pastures: nor had the land ever been associated in my mind with physical labour. As a result it became for me the playground of my most pleasurable fancies. I was an incurable daydreamer, but the daydreams I indulged in while walking were always alive to my actual surroundings, so that a rook passing overhead and calling became an omen, and the shade of a weatherbeaten hawthorn was a refuge in my mental travelling. My daydreams were of adventure, of heroism, of extraordinary obstacle courses which I must complete, of gypsies, of circuses, of strange fellow travellers met on obscure paths in the course of obscure missions. Brandy was my protector and guide in these dangerous exploits while the tall elms, broad oaks, lonely alders and above all every curve, twist and mood of the beautiful Stour were the landmarks of my adventuring.

I had put *Albion's Dream* out of my mind over Christmas. But once the festivities were over I got out the game and ceremoniously polished the beads, cleaned out and repaired the box and tried to decide how I could experiment with the discovery that I had made, and of which I was now certain in my mind, that the landscape of the game was derived from the landscape of the Blackmoor Vale and the surrounding ridges of hills. I bought myself the local OS map and laid it out on the floor of my room to pore over it. I found further correspondences: there was a village called Hermitage in the correct position; the Holy Well appeared on the map as the village of Holywell; the Coast was in the right place for the Dorset coastline.

I decided to continue my investigations with a visit to one of the fortresses close to home. But even now I was frightened of anti-climax. I decided therefore that I must play first and then follow whatever movements were dictated by the fall of the dice and the appearance of the cards.

Having no one to play with I cheated a little. My brother Ben at that time was about five years old, just the age to join in any game without the need to understand in any more than the simplest way what was going on. He was within the family, after all, and I could make his moves for him. I knew that this was not in keeping with the true spirit of the instructions, but it gave me a thrill to feel myself alone with the game, and not to have to share all the secrets with Hadley, or listen to his strictures, wise though they might be.

I decided that if the game proved to have any more nasty surprises in store, I would simply fold it up and put it away. I was not prepared to have other people getting hurt or falling ill again on my account. In the present surroundings, far from Hadley, Tyson, Tom, Avery, with no one but myself to consider, I was drawn to consider the game more as an extension of my daydreamed adventures than as a source of actual power capable of making dents on reality.

I thought of Tom's words, the ones that had so impressed Hadley, about the magician 'making his own decisions as to who can get away with what'. I cast myself in the role of superior magician, bending the rules to suit my purposes. All the fears and frailnesses that we had known while playing the game at school, I attributed to Hadley, as if he had been the weak and vacillating one, holding me back from my true potential.

I had become very superstitious, acutely aware of anything that could be read as an omen. I found an old black coat with a scarlet lining that we had once used for dressing up. I kept the game on the highest pile on the highest shelf and when I took it down I avoided touching it with my left, or sinister, hand. For my session with Ben, I chose a bright, clear, sunny Tuesday morning, as Tuesdays were always favourable to me. I put a chair against the door of my room to avoid any intrusion by my mother. The house was anyway fairly empty, my father away in London, my elder sister returned to Plymouth.

The game began. Ben showed great interest in all the pieces and had to be reminded continually not to pick them up and move them around at random. But he was quite attentive and soon got the idea that there was some kind of movement towards the centre and that there were battles to be fought on the way, both of which he found highly satisfying. Partly to keep his interest, for I didn't wish to risk losing him and not being able to continue the game, and partly to limit the game's possibilities, I played both our hands cautiously, concentrating on amassing tokens rather than on speeding towards the numinous central regions. With the Merchant and the Hangman I occupied the Rings. Ben drew the Soldier and then Christ. Normally one would discard a mage so early in the game and draw again, hoping for a warrior, and I explained this. But Ben had taken such a strong and immediate fancy to the picture on the Christ card that he refused to part with it, threatening a tearful outburst when I started to insist. There was nothing for it and he kept the Christ.

Soon after, he drew the mighty Thor and moved to the Second Kingdom where he occupied Barrow Hill. Then I, too, drew a warrior, the ageing Pellinore, and occupied the adjacent position. This fortress was called Dome Hill, which I had also found on the OS map. From these positions we fought a long battle centred on the control of the ford which provided the passage into the Third

THE BARROW AND THE DOME

Kingdom. By various sallies and raids, both of us collected a goodly pile of beads.

Then Ben threw a series of very high scores and Thor, with Christ, moved into the Third Kingdom and occupied the Healing Stone. My own pieces were intact, however, and I followed him on my next move.

At this point my mother's voice called us from below. Anyway it seemed a good place to stop. The game was not over but I decided it could be continued another time. When Ben left the room I made a note of the positions on the board, and put the board away. I felt very pleased. The game had clearly indicated the two hills as the direction of my first explorations.

As the hills were so close to home, I decided not to cycle but to walk. That way I could take Brandy with me. I set off early the next morning equipped, at my mother's insistence, with a small rucksack containing something to eat for lunch. I was in high spirits. The morning was fine and cloudless and Brandy was more than usually excited with that strange instinct that dogs have for something out of the ordinary.

It was a bit further than I had imagined, and by the time I reached Barrow Hill I was already tired. It was only nine o'clock but I sat and ate my 'lunch' while I debated which of the two hills to climb. Barrow Hill lay above me, the grassy ramparts of the fort curling round the hill more like the artistry of some ancient Cyclopean architect than the fortifications of warlike tribes. I knew the place well. It was a favourite goal of family excursions. It is a friendly, bright, open hillside fringed with generous beeches. The Dome was a mile further on, less familiar to me and darker somehow though smaller in scale. I wanted to climb Barrow Hill, but I felt that as I had occupied the Dome in the game of the day before, then it was my proper destination, and so thither I reluctantly turned.

A breeze sprang up from the south west, blowing against me. I noticed now that the horizon was ringed with dark clouds. Brandy had finished his earlier forays away in front of me and now stuck obediently to my heels. I saw him looking first towards Barrow Hill then towards me as if to suggest that we should go there, but my mind was made up and I ignored him.

The path up the side of Dome Hill was muddy. Once I slipped and received a thick coating of mud up one side of my trousers and jacket. I was thirsty, and by the time I reached the summit the sun had gone and the dark clouds had rolled in from the west. Looking back towards Barrow Hill I saw it for a moment still bathed in sunshine, before it too was covered in shadow.

The summit of Dome Hill is a gently rounded hilltop covered in a coarse turf. As far as I could see Brandy and I were quite alone. I felt depressed, and so apparently did Brandy. He even ignored a couple of rabbits who sped off down the hill.

What next? Should I wait here for something to happen, for somebody to come? I decided, arbitrarily, that I would wait half an hour. From where I sat I could see Shillingstone Hill and, beyond it, Bulbarrow. Somewhere beyond that were the Gap and the Tout, the landmarks that stood at the entrance to the last Kingdom. I hoped that I would have the sense to stay away from there, but I was unaccountably nervous, as if I were not truly in control of my own actions. Hadn't I wished with all my heart to climb Barrow Hill and hadn't the course of the game forced me to come to the shadowy Dome? Was I free to go where I liked? I thought about this carefully.

According to the game, I should now proceed to the ford, which was the nearest entrance to the Third Kingdom. This clearly meant the ford over the Stour, which I could see directly below me. I decided not to wait for the rest of the half hour and not to go to the ford at all, but to descend the hill in exactly the opposite direction. I felt pleased with this decision, as if I were casting off some insidious influence, and, calling Brandy, I began trotting off down the hill.

About half way down I saw a figure crossing the road below me and starting up through the field that I was about to enter. I climbed the fence and saw the figure more clearly. It was a dark-haired, red-faced, broad-shouldered man, and, I now noticed, he held between his hands a piece of black plastic hose which he was flexing ominously. When I was close enough to see the expression on his face, I could see that he was furious.

How they scare me, these red-faced, thick-necked muscular men with veins that knot and bulge below their ears, who sweat too much and who spend the whole of their lives looking for a quarrel.

I thought of running. But I couldn't understand why I should run away, why this man was so furiously angry with me. So I stood nervously where I was and waited for him. He was flexing his length of hose more and more menacingly. He obviously meant me to understand exactly what he intended to do with it, but while he was still out of striking range, I called out a polite "Good Morning." Or at least it was supposed to be a polite good morning though it came out as a sort of strangled groan.

"What the Hell are you doing here," the man yelled. His voice was like the rest of him, violent.

"I... I was just taking the dog for a walk. Didn't mean any harm, sir."

"Just taking the bloody dog for a walk. And where? ON MY LAND, that's where. I've a good mind to..."

But he didn't finish and he stopped flexing his hose. I think he found me a little more kempt and polite than he had expected. And of course he had liked the 'sir'. They always do.

"Where's the footpath here, I'd like to know. Where's the bloody public footpath?"

I made no reply.

"It's over that way, sonny, the way you've come from. That's where it is."

He pointed to the other side of the hill. "And that's where you're going right now. At the double." He started towards me again.

"I'm dreadfully sorry, sir. You see, on my map..."

"I don't give a damn for your map. I'm the bloody mapmaker

around here, OK? People march over my farm as if they own the place, leave the gates open, let their dogs chase my sheep, trample on the corn, do what they bloody well like and then tell me that on their map…"

I was backing away up the hill.

"Go on. Scram. SCRAM." He made a sudden move as if to strike me with that unpleasant little weapon of his. I needed no further encouragement. I turned and ran.

The going was slippery and steep and the incline was quite sharp, and there was the fence to negotiate as well, but I made good time. The man was still watching me as I disappeared over the crown of the hill. I didn't stop until I'd descended the other side, breathless and tearful. He'd frightened me, that angry, ugly landowner, but that wasn't the worst. I had been shown as clearly as if it had been spelt out for me, that there was no going against the injunctions of the game.

I was trapped.

CHAPTER SIX

THE DUNGEON

I might then have left the game for good, but there was the instruction that a game, once started, must be finished. I could have ignored the rule, of course, but something had happened to me up on the Dome that morning when the clouds had come over so suddenly, as if they were clouds blown over the horizon of my own mind. I had been blighted by a shadow, and the red-faced landowner was a product of that blight, not the cause of it. A definite lingering nervousness began to afflict me. I noticed it especially at dusk. I felt restless and anxious. Once or twice it was as if I had caught a glimpse of an actual batlike shape behind me, although when I turned round there was nothing to be seen.

There was no one I could talk to about what I was feeling. My mother would have been as solicitous as ever, but in the end she would have taken me to the doctor — worse than useless.

I examined what had happened that morning step by step. I decided that I must have picked up whatever it was the moment I had opted against Barrow Hill. After all, my instinct had been sure that it was a favourable place and that the Dome in some way was not. By making the decision I did, I had put myself at the mercy of the powers of the game: that was the closest I could get to an explanation.

THE DUNGEON

You mustn't think that this notion of a 'friendly' or 'unfriendly' place was new to me, for since my earliest years I had been aware of these atmospheres and I had always taken them seriously. Houses especially. If it happened to me that I was to stay for a night in a house that struck me as 'unfriendly' it was a real ordeal for me. And in my long ramblings and fishing expeditions I was unashamedly superstitious. Not liking the particular way that the shadow of a tree fell on the ground, I would make a detour to avoid it; the shape of a bough above me while I was fishing would cause me to move. Often I would read the fortunes of the day ahead in certain signs provided by the clouds, the leaves and the moods of the breeze. So when I had ignored my instinct in favour of Barrow Hill and gone instead to the Dome it had indeed been unusual, perhaps unprecedented for me. Yet nothing was really explained. This oppressive burden on my spirits, what was it really?

Whatever the answer, I had to continue the game with Ben. I was moody and nervous when I got the board out again and the morning was overcast. Ben didn't feel like playing so I spoke roughly to him, forcing him to agree. During the game he sat sullenly.

I set up the pieces as they had been. Ben's position was the stronger but I discarded the Merchant and drew Galahad, my favourite warrior, and then one of the guides, Hod. With them I occupied the Dungeon in the Third Kingdom. Ben was at the Healing Stone. I would have preferred to settle into these fortresses and to spend the game raiding for tokens, sending out spies and waging a war of attrition. But Ben already had a mage, Christ, and when he also drew a guide, Puck, he could hardly avoid moving into the Fourth Kingdom. He negotiated the Gap and took up position on the Tout, removing most of my tokens and defeating Pellinore on the way. This at least had the effect of cheering him up – seeing the large pile of beads in his possession.

"When I get there," he said, pointing to the very centre of the board, "I'll get all the beads, won't I?"

I laughed, knowing that the centre was still a long way off, but I couldn't help thinking of the possibility, remote though it might be, that my little brother, in his first game, would do what neither Hadley nor I, nor apparently my father or my uncle Jack, had managed to do in a hundred games.

On his next turn he drew Hermes, and Christ cast a spell over Devilish. My own part in the game was by now largely irrelevant. He could easily have turned on me now and finished me off, but his position in the Fourth Kingdom was so strong that I knew he must try for the Fifth. I made the decision for him that I would have made for myself, trading in his tokens to buy him another mage or guide. This time he drew Merlin, which meant that he now held Thor, Christ, Merlin, Puck and Hermes.

To enter the Fifth Kingdom, you first have to control the winds. Then you have to find the entrance. This is not always in the same place, and the odds against finding it are high, but Ben could seemingly do nothing wrong. Within a few goes, he found the Caer Sidh and was able to do battle with the Dragon Time. The form of this battle is simple. The Dragon can choose between a number of different disguises, with corresponding weapons. The crucial act on the part of the seeker is to guess in which role the Dragon will appear, and to have the appropriate card ready to meet him. Ben had a warrior, two mages and two guides. I explained to him what he had to do and left him to make the guesses. He chose Christ, his favourite card. The Dragon was then turned over. He wore a cloak of wizardry. Christ was his match.

These two cards were returned to their places. Ben chose again. Thor. This time the Dragon appeared as himself, the Great Worm. The warrior was the correct choice.

The third time Ben again chose Christ as his champion. Again the Dragon wore the wizard's garments. He had to stand aside and allow Ben to enter the Fifth Kingdom, which he did.

Somehow I expected this final move to be accompanied by a sign from the world around us. I looked out of the window, where I saw the clouds were clearing and the sky brightening from the west. Some jackdaws were circling the church. One of the ponies looked up from its grazing in the paddock. My mother hove into sight carrying a small garden fork.

I looked back at Ben. He was sitting by the game, carefully collecting the tokens in a tidy pile in front of him. When he finished, he began collecting the entire set of cards, then the pieces. At the end he was sat there surrounded by every piece of the game with an expression of the most complete satisfaction. He looked up at me and beamed. What struck me at that moment, and what

THE DUNGEON

I remembered later, was the complete absence of smugness in that look of fulfilment, as if he was enjoying the fruits offered him by the world, but without the least suspicion that he deserved them.

My shadow haunted the following days. Dusk especially became charged with a nameless threat. It was as if the game had pushed me into another more ominous dimension, in which my life was no longer fully under my own control and which infected even the everyday familiarities I had always taken for granted.

For the first time in my conscious life I felt there was nobody I could turn to, and it seems to me now that it is at just such a moment that the innocence of childhood disappears for ever.

Even sleep scared me. I feared I would get lost in some huge mythic dream and never escape.

One night, as I fought against sleep, and as it came all the same, it seemed that a kind of bolt snapped shut in my brain and I was wide awake again, full of a sudden alien clarity.

I made my decision. I would stay awake until dawn. I would pack my rucksack with a few things, and I would set off by bicycle for Dungeon Hill. I was convinced that if I did not confront this evil that was creeping up on me, I was in danger of losing my sanity.

The game had left me at the Dungeon and I must meet myself there.

I couldn't wait for the first light. At five o'clock I crept downstairs and found some bread and cheese and chocolate

THE DUNGEON

digestive biscuits in the kitchen. I left a scribbled note, 'Gone fishing early. Back later'. As I walked through to the back door, I passed Brandy who barely stirred in his sleep.

Outside it was freezing cold and by the time I cycled to the end of the drive I felt icy. Countless times during the seven or eight mile ride I came near to turning back, but I was frozen to the bike and frozen to my purpose.

It was a hilly, difficult journey and I was unsure of my way. I had the map with me, and a torch, but I was afraid to stop for a look. Huge oaks bent over me and threatened me with their leafless fingers. The road seemed more like a tunnel.

At last, after struggling up Bulbarrow, I saw a glimmer of light in the east. I passed a cow byre with a light on and a bicycle outside. A milk lorry thundered past me with the empty milk churns crashing against each other. I reached the village below Dungeon Hill and the eastern horizon was etched against an apricot sky. I got off and tried to force some feeling back into my numbed hands. I finally managed to get the torch pointed at the right part of the map and found the dotted red track that was the footpath. I was not going to risk a repeat of what had happened on Dome Hill.

I found the path and hid my bicycle in the brambles by the stile. As I climbed, day broke properly and it was light enough for me to see my way. I began to feel cheerful again, proud, even, to be so far from home by sunrise. The sky was cloudless and the dewdrops sparkled here and there. The way led up to a ring of mighty beeches standing on some kind of rampart. Strange how my fears had fled, how the night before now seemed only a nightmare.

When I reached the rampart and climbed it, a great oval field was revealed to me, surrounded by the tall trees. It was a wonderful citadel, atop a symmetrical hill, an ideal refuge for men and beasts in any age. I felt utterly at my ease, in possession of the stronghold at the start of what promised to be a beautiful day. I sat and watched and thought. It was as if I could sense the healing powers of nature all around me, making me feel strong and confident. Next to where I sat I found a perfectly straight stick, bare in places where somebody had begun to strip off its bark. I took out my penknife to finish the job. The stick was too long for a staff, more like a lance. It fitted my grip exactly. Thus armed I began a tour of the battlements, watching the smoke rising from the chimneys of the houses below, and a herd of cows issuing from a barn and spreading out slowly over the lower slopes. Their breath formed little clouds of silvery moisture.

There I was in my own castle, lance in hand. I was Galahad!

I had always loved Galahad above all of Arthur's knights, more than Lancelot who was untrue, more than the aged Pellinore, more than Perceval or Gawain. Galahad was the youngest and the brightest. He alone had looked on the Holy Grail itself.

How stupid I had become with the game, putting myself at the mercy of its black aspects, when I could always have been Galahad in his citadel. How puny seemed the Friendly Hangman! How far away seemed the woodland Puck! I wished Tom could see me now. This was a real camp, high and unassailable.

THE DUNGEON

I soon became involved in one of my elaborate daydreams, scheming with my advisers, organising my defences, leading dangerous sorties to spy on my enemies down on the plain.

I grew hungry and ate. Then as the day warmed up, I felt sleepy and decided to rest for a while. The sleep that had seemed such an ordeal to me the night before crept over me gently, gently.

When I awoke it was to find myself in shadow. A tall figure stood over me. He held a staff in one hand and his face was hidden against the bright sunlight. I might have been shocked, but something in his bearing was unmistakably friendly.

"Hello," he said. His voice was deep and sonorous. It did not sound quite English.

I got to my feet and saw the man properly.

"Hello."

He was very tall and old. He had a bright ruddy face with a large gleaming forehead. He wore glasses and was dressed in a battered pair of corduroy trousers together with a jersey that had clearly seen better days. From his shoulders hung a dark blue cloak.

"I didn't mean to wake you," he went on in that mellifluous, resonant voice, "but it's not often I come across sleeping children on my morning walks, and I just wondered whether…well, whether you were all right."

He seemed a little embarrassed, thus to be enquiring about my welfare. I liked him immediately.

"Oh, I'm OK," I said. "I must have dropped off for a few minutes."

"A good while, I should say," he said. "I've been here myself for ten minutes or so."

He spread his cloak behind him and sat on a log, as if prepared for a conversation.

"Would you like a cheese sandwich?" I asked him.

"Well, yes I would. That would be very nice."

He took the crumpled offering and bit into it with obvious pleasure. He chewed for a while and took another bite. I was surprised that so old a man should take such large bites.

"There, er…there doesn't seem to be any cheese in this one," he said apologetically.

"Oh dear. Oh I'm dreadfully sorry. There was some cheese, I'm sure." I hunted in my rucksack and there, sure enough, was the errant slice of cheese now decorated with grime from the recesses of my bag. I offered it to him anyway.

"Thankyou," he said seriously. He took the cheese, dusted off the worst of the grime and placed it in its rightful position again. Again that huge mouthful.

"Excellent," he said, "Excellent cheese."

He finished the sandwich. "I hope there's some more left for you."

"Yes," I lied. "I've just eaten anyway."

"Good," he said, and got out his pipe. "And now tell me how you come to be up here asleep so early in the morning. Part of a long adventure, no doubt."

THE DUNGEON

I looked at him quickly, but there was nothing on his face but the most friendly curiosity, and nothing in his attitude except the ease of someone with plenty of time on his hands.

Looking back on this moment in my story—a moment, although I did not then know it, that marked a turning point for me—I am surprised that it was so easy for me to confide in an aged man whom I had only just met. But something in the extraordinary circumstances of our meeting and some instinct that this was an unusually kind old man, and perhaps above all, an overwhelming need to confide in somebody, anybody, decided me to tell my tale.

Parts of it I left out: how the game had come into my possession, and what I had learned of the experiences of my father and uncle. But as I got into my stride, I found myself telling all the rest, about Hadley, Tyson, Puck and Pellinore. In fact I became so absorbed in what I was saying that it was not until I got to the game with Ben and to my visit to Dome Hill that I remembered where I was and who I was talking to. Suddenly I decided I'd said enough. I had not told the old man my sense of being under a black spell—it was still too close to talk about.

I think he guessed there was more, but he didn't press me to go on. He was silent for a long time, longer than one is allowed to remain silent in so- called polite conversation. I began to feel uncomfortable, but I didn't want to move for risk of disturbing him.

Finally he brought his gaze back from whatever distance he had

THE DUNGEON

been contemplating and let it rest on me. There was no trace of a smile now, but there was a peculiarly penetrating look in his eyes. He got up.

"Well, it's time we continued on our separate ways, I think, young man. I've enjoyed meeting you." He held out his hand and we shook hands. His clasp was so strong it almost hurt. Rather abruptly he turned to go.

"But wait. Please sir, wait a minute."

He turned immediately as if he'd been expecting me to call him back.

"What should I do? I mean…I thought you might be able to advise me."

"Oh, I think you know what to do with the game," he said, with a smile. "The best thing to do is stop playing it. You know that."

"Should I throw it away?"

"No," he said thoughtfully. "No, I don't think I would do that if I were you. You see you might regret it later on. Nothing is ever wholly good or wholly bad in this world, it depends on what we make of things, that's all."

"Can I walk with you a little way?"

"Of course. I'd be pleased to have your company. But I cover considerable distances on these rambles of mine, you know. I was heading towards Nettlecombe. I wouldn't want to take you out of your way."

"Well, I have to go back for my bike," I said. "But we could walk together until then."

THE DUNGEON

We walked mostly in silence, he with the staff and I with my lance. The path was narrow and we had to go in single file, but I was happy following the old man like this, even at his surprising speed, which had me almost trotting to keep up. When we got to the road he prepared to turn right. My bike was the other way.

"I'd better leave you now," I said.

"Farewell," he said gravely, holding out his hand.

"Will you tell me one thing?" I asked him.

"If I can," he replied.

"Did you believe what I told you about the game? You didn't think I was making it up?"

"Oh no," he said immediately. "I would never have thought that."

"But most adults, you know, they don't believe in things like that."

"In my experience of the world," he said, "just about everything is possible for the right person at the right time. It's better to believe things, I've found."

"Yes," I said.

"Oh, if you should ever feel like having another little chat, just come to my village and ask for me. They all know me there."

"I'd like that. But you didn't tell me your name."

"Nor I did. My name's Hodman. Owen Hodman. And yours?"

I told him and we parted.

What a terrific old man, I was thinking. What a good time we'd have if all adults treated children as he did. He never made me feel small. I'd told him all those incredible things and he'd believed me. I would certainly go and see him, as soon as I could think of an excuse. Something to take him, that's all I'd need. A gift. What on earth could I take him though? A hat? A walking stick? Yes, that was it, I'd find a marvellous walking stick for him, I'd cut it myself and strip it and polish it, and I'd cycle to his house and give it to him. And I'd tell him what I hadn't told him today, about my father and Jack and about the awful pursuing shadow and the fear. I mustn't forget his name, though. What was it?

And only then did it strike me. I had been so pleased by the old man – like a brand new and ideal godfather he was – that I had not really noticed his name. Hodman.

He was the Hod, of course.

I thought back to the game with Ben. I had drawn Galahad and occupied the Dungeon. There I had drawn Hod. Mr. Hodman was on his way to Nettlecombe, where the Tout was. Nettlecombe Tout.

I began to run towards my bike. If I could catch up with him, I could proceed to the Tout with Hod as my guide. I saw his remark about stopping the game in a new light. He must have meant that I didn't need the game any more. I didn't need to play it because I was in it. I had occupied the Dungeon with Galahad and now I could go to the Tout with Hod. There I would be in the Fourth Kingdom and close to the hub of the mystery. Suddenly the thought of the Fifth Kingdom held no terrors for me, but only the promise of an absorbing resolution.

THE DUNGEON

I should have realised, though, knowing what I did, that the Fourth Kingdom was not for me that day. The game had not ordained it. I rode up and down the road and even followed a short way up the track I thought the old man would have taken, but he was nowhere to be seen.

I arrived back home tired and hungry, but dusk brought no return of the fear. For the rest of the holidays the game stayed on its shelf.

CHAPTER SEVEN

DOCTOR DEATH

HOWEVER many times I returned to school, I never got over the sense of loss and abandonment which overcame me on the first day of term.

Everything had been scrubbed and Detolled and Harpicked and french polished and the school smelt like something between a hospital and a new police station. Thank God for the new boys, who looked so pale and awkward that the sight of them made the rest of us feel like old hands. Besides, I was twelve years old, a sixth former, a member of the first eleven and Tyson's favourite, what excuse had I to be shy or lonely?

Hadley sought me out as soon as I arrived. Had I brought the game, he wanted to know. Had I been playing during the holidays?

It had occurred to me to keep secret from Hadley the events of the last fortnight, but in fact I found myself only too eager to share my experiences, and I told him about the landscape of the game and about everything that had happened since we last played. He listened attentively until I finished.

"You threw away a golden opportunity, Yeoman."

I was a bit nettled at this, but he had more to say.

"You were wrong to play with your brother, because he wasn't fully aware of the game. What you were doing was playing against yourself. That's where you picked up the bad spell. One part of you chose Barrow Hill, the other chose the Dome. You were split and so you were vulnerable. That's what happened. But the game gave you an amazing chance and you threw it away."

"I thought I did pretty well. I bet you wouldn't have gone all the way to Dungeon Hill before dawn. It's all very well to criticise me, but would you have done any better, I wonder?"

"Perhaps not, but I've always taken the game more seriously than you, and anyway I've been working at it too."

"What do you mean?"

We were sitting side by side in the classroom of the sixth form. As usual Hadley's desk was at the top, in the corner. He opened his desk and drew out a package. "Here's *my* game," he said.

He opened the wrappings and took out a board, some counters.

"I made my own version," he said.

And there it was. Not as beautiful as the original and without, of course, the same feeling of age, but nevertheless complete and a faithful replica.

My first instinct was to be angry.

"You had no right," I said.

"There was nothing in the instructions," he said, "nothing to say that a duplicate shouldn't be made. Besides, you had started to get jealous of the game. It was always you who decided when it should be played and when it shouldn't. D'you know where that left me? I was just as involved in what happened to Pellinore and to Tom, but it was only you who could decide when to play next, and you were not playing it properly."

"I was."

"You were not. Something in you has always refused to admit that the game influences people's lives, and that makes you careless."

"That's not true. It may have been true before, but I've learnt a lot, Hadley. I've been badly scared, and I've learnt a lot."

"Yes," he said, "I can see that. But that's now and I'm talking about then."

He picked up his version of the game and held it against himself as if challenging me to make an issue of it.

I watched him a moment, deciding how I would react.

"Let's have a look," I said. He handed me the game and I opened it. It had been made with amazing skill and patience. Of all the people I know, only Hadley could have created such a careful copy.

"It's brilliant," I said.

"Thankyou."

Perhaps the chief reason that I didn't make a fuss about Hadley's copy was my unspoken conviction that the secret of the game's power lay in the dice. Without the original dice, I felt, the game was indeed just a game.

I flicked through the character cards. They resembled the originals in many respects but the faces represented Hadley's own ideas. The Puck card, for example, had obviously been made with Tom in mind. But the greatest shock was Galahad.

"Why have you drawn him like this?" I asked.

Hadley was watching me carefully. "What do you mean?" he said.

"Well, this is me, isn't it?"

"I didn't do it on purpose, but I just found myself thinking of you as I drew it."

I had not mentioned to Hadley my partiality for Galahad. Nor, up to the moment on Dungeon Hill, had I identified myself with him.

"Anyway," he went on, "by what you've just told me, it sounds as if I was on the right track."

"I suppose so, yes."

"You don't mind, do you?"

"No, I don't mind, but…"

I didn't finish the sentence. I didn't mind – I even felt flattered – but it was another way in which the realm of the game had closed in on my reality and it made me uncomfortable.

"Have you worked out what all this is really about?" I asked him.

"If you mean how it operates, no, I don't know," he said. "But I have been thinking about how we can use it, since we're not in Dorset, I mean. If we were there we would have to try for the centre, wouldn't we? But as it is, I'm sure we've first got to stop thinking of the game as being played against each other, and start exploring the possibilities of changing the things we want to change."

"What do you mean?"

"Tyson, for example. I'm sure we can put a stop to him."

"Maybe. But supposing he starts getting seriously ill, or has an accident, or meets Death? You know that in the end it's the dice that decides the course of the game. We can't control that. We'll get ourselves into a mess again and this time we may not be able to get out of it."

Hadley argued that, with proper caution, and without the element of competition which, he said, had been distorting our games, we would be able to protect our characters from the worst fates, but he couldn't convince me, and I announced my intention of not playing at all for the time being. If I refused to join in I knew that he couldn't play, even with his new set, because no one else in the school could possibly be described as 'within the family'.

So both versions of the game remained idle for the first two weeks of term and I saw little of Hadley.

Then one morning I met Death coming down the corridor. I knew him instantly. I drew quickly back into the doorway of one of the dormitories as he passed. He saw me there and smiled at me, with a slightly puzzled expression, as if surprised, as well he might have been because he must have seen the look of astonishment written on my face.

He was younger than I would have expected, but he was a perfect replica of the Death card; the same long, hollow cheeks, the same prominent jaw and brow, the same deepset, searching eyes.

He was carrying what looked like a Doctor's bag. Oddly enough, this did not strike me as incongruous.

He went on past, but it was some moments before I cautiously emerged into the corridor again. The figure had already, it seemed, turned the corner at the end.

I followed cautiously, dreading to catch up with him. By the time I reached the gym, he was just leaving it through the door at the other end. Even at that distance, and seeing him from behind, his head was unmistakably that of Death. I arrived at the window by the main school entrance in time to see him opening the boot of a small red car in the forecourt. It seemed a puny sort of car for such an ominous figure. As he went to get into the driver's seat, he turned back towards the school and I was sure that he caught sight of me watching him. For an instant our eyes met, then I ducked out of sight.

At that moment Hadley walked out of the sixth form, in the company of Abbott. "What on earth are you up to, Yeoman?" he said, seeing me crouched below the window. I put my finger to my lips and pointed urgently outside. Hadley came to look out and I stood cautiously to join him. The man was backing his car up in order to drive out of the gate. He was quite close to us, his face in profile. As he drove off he turned again to where we were standing and again I caught his glance on me. This time it was too late to duck, and for a clear instant he seemed to look at me carefully. I knew that he would recognise me another time.

"Blimey," whispered Hadley beside me, "it's Death."

You see, it wasn't just my imagination.

Abbott came up beside us and peered shortsightedly out of the window.

"What are you two looking at?" he said, taking off his glasses and wiping them. "You look as if you'd seen a ghost." He returned his glasses to their normal position and peered out again. "That man in the red car," he said, "that's the new school doctor. He's replacing Doctor Rogers. Much younger and more competent, I should say," he remarked in his judicious manner.

"What's his name?" Hadley asked.

"Dr. Finn, I believe. No, Fell. Dr. Fell."

Immediately the old rhyme came into my mind:

>I do not love thee, Dr. Fell
>
>The reason why I cannot tell
>
>But this I know and know full well
>
>I do not love thee, Dr. Fell.

We got rid of Abbott as soon as we could. Hadley sent him off to look for something in the library.

"You saw him, then," I blurted out as soon as we were alone.

"I saw him alright. There's no mistaking him. You wanted to stop the game, but you couldn't."

"What do you mean?" I knew perfectly well what he meant, but I didn't want to believe it.

"I meant that whether we play or not, the game goes on. That's what I've been trying to tell you. The geography of the game is not limited to one place. Come here and I'll show you something. I wanted to show you before but you weren't interested."

He led the way to the sixth form and I followed him to his desk. He took out some kind of a map.

"Look here. This is the school and the grounds. When you told me about Dome Hill and Dungeon Castle and the rest, I began working on a theory of my own. Look. This is Tyson's study. Tyson is the Hangman, right? And his favourite spot is the Rings. Now over here is Tom's place in the woods. That would be the Camp, where Puck is to be found. Here is Avery's house, and that would be the Hermitage. OK? Now if you draw the five rings something like I've done here, you'll see that these places correspond to the positions on the board."

I looked, and he was right.

"But you've only marked three places," I said.

"Yes, but that's because we've only discovered three characters. Hold on a moment. The Doctor, if we put him in the Sick Bay—that's where he belongs, isn't it? We'll put him here." He found the place on his map. "And isn't that the Dole where you always meet Death?"

He was right again. There was a long pause while we both digested this piece of news.

"You see, we'll have to play again," he said. "There's nothing for it."

But I still opposed him. I argued that we would only get ourselves into worse trouble. Hadley got quite cross with me, but he was too gentle for real anger, and my will was the stronger. I would not play, I told him.

"You will, you know," he said. "You'll have to."

It was a chill, draughty place, the school in February. A cold spell set in and the usual run of colds, coughs and 'flu broke out. One morning in prayers I noticed that the assembly was quite depleted.

After prayers Tyson motioned for the staff to remain and we could tell that an announcement was coming. There was the usual expectant silence when something out of the ordinary was in the air.

"I'm sorry to report," said Tyson weightily, "that we are currently the victims of a particularly nasty outbreak of Asian influenza." He pronounced the word "Asian" as if he was thinking of Japanese war atrocities and centuries of Chinese trickery. "We are not alone in this. A new and alien virus is abroad and even our most stringent precautions have not been able to safeguard us. Twenty-five boys have been diagnosed as having succumbed to this virus. The Sick Bay is full, and the worst cases have been sent to recuperate at home. Two or three schools in the neighbourhood have actually taken the step of returning most of their pupils to their homes and are operating only a skeleton service for those remaining. In consultation with the school doctor I have decided that such an extreme course of action is unnecessary and that we at this school have the resources and the discipline to cope with our own problems. However, certain measures are necessary, and, as from today, Sunny Glade and Keeper's Cottage are designated sick rooms. The boys from these dormitories will be allocated beds in other dormitories. The number of classes will be reduced to four, and the details of these changes will be given separately to form masters. There will be no classes as such today and all boys will be inspected by the school doctor, who, together with Miss Daphne, will give immunising injections to those boys who are still fit. These injections can only be given to boys who are in a satisfactory state of health, so it is important that all headaches, coughs, and colds be notified to Miss Daphne or to Doctor Fell himself. As from tomorrow morning, classes and other activities will resume, and I trust that the school will prove worthy of my confidence, by refusing to join the ranks of the defeated."

It was a formal speech for Tyson, the sort that he reserved for the hearing of staff, parents and the general public. I had no doubt that we would get another, earthier version of his feelings at some later date.

That afternoon I took my turn in the queue outside Miss Daphne's little dispensary. Hadley was with me. We didn't speak of it, but both of us were nervous at the prospect of meeting Dr. Fell, quite apart from my own private horror at the thought of an injection. The rumour was out that a number of boys were found already to have contracted the first symptoms of the 'alien virus' and were being whisked immediately into quarantine. The Glen had been added to the list of sick rooms.

I went in before Hadley. The doctor was evidently tired. His face was even more cadaverous than when I had seen him a few days before. There were two or three boys ahead of me within the narrow dispensary and I had time to observe the doctor closely. He was indeed a young man, younger than my father, I guessed, and handsome in an angular sort of way. His skin was surprisingly tanned. His movements were deft and skilful. To each boy he made a number of kindly remarks, chatting to distract them from the actual injection. His voice was pleasant enough, although he clipped his vowels and his lips were thin. Not one of the boys, I noticed, watched while the needle pierced his skin.

When it came to my turn, he looked up at me and smiled.

"Ah," he said. "My friend at the window."

Miss Daphne looked round from her business at the shelves.

"Oh, that's Yeoman, doctor," she said. She had always liked me, and had even found herself acting as my protector from time to time, ever since I'd arrived at the school, not quite seven years old, and something less than four feet. I had been the littlest of her little ones, and she remembered it.

"Well, you seem all right, Yeoman, but let's have a look anyway," and I opened my mouth and said "Ahh" a couple of times, and the doctor peered closely into my eyes, so closely that I couldn't see him, I just had the impression of this long face jutting up towards me. It was suddenly as if the moment was frozen, with this pleasant voice saying I don't know what from a long way away and the only sensation that I had was of Death come close, not frightening or morbid, or ghastly, but almost reassuring.

I looked down at my arm in time to see the needle hover over my flesh and then plunge, with the slightest prick, into me. Then everything came back into focus.

"Your father's Will Yeoman, isn't he?" he was saying.

"Yes," I said, surprised.

"I knew your family years ago. I knew your Uncle Jack."

Then my sleeve was rolled down and I was out of his presence.

I waited for Hadley in the sixth form. When he came in he was more than usually pale and excited.

"I smelt the evil of him," he said.

This puzzled me. I myself had sensed no evil.

"Look at you," he went on. "He didn't frighten you or anything. You damn well liked him, didn't you?"

I made no answer.

"What am I to make of you," he said. "Sometimes it seems to me that you belong *on the other side*. First you get sorry for Tyson, then you're actually pleased when Tom gets kicked out, and now you come away from meeting Dr. Death himself, and you're smiling all over your face."

This was a bit much, and yet... And yet it had always been like that in my life. I never seemed to belong either on one side or the other. I remember that one day I set a trap for a mouse that had been bothering my mother by invading her larder – one of those traps that catch the animal alive – and before I went to bed I heard the tell-tale snapping of the gate of the trap. I took a torch and went to see what I had caught. It was a tiny mouse, clean as a whistle, with a coat shiny and perfectly groomed, and it was zooming around the little cage trying every wire, every gap, to see how it could escape, putting its teeth around every strut and every bar and — what impressed me most — never stopping in its attempts to find a way out. I knew it would keep going like that all night and I felt sorry for it. Not only that: it reminded me of myself.

In the morning I took out the cage and called the cat and opened the trap and watched. I heard the crunch of those perfect, tiny bones as they cracked in the cat's mouth and, honestly, I suffered no remorse.

Hadley had more to say.

"Yeoman, I've got a sore throat. I didn't tell the doctor, but he saw it anyway. I've got to go into quarantine."

"I'm sorry about that, Hadley. Does it hurt?"

"No, it doesn't hurt, but it means I'm getting the 'flu and I'll be in the Sick Bay for a week or so, and if we're going to play the game, we have to play it now."

"We'll play when you get out."

Hadley was silent for a moment. Then he reached for a book on the shelves by his desk. I knew the book: it was called *The Arthurian Romances*.

"Listen." He found the page he was looking for. "To Galahad alone it was given to find and hold the Grail, but Galahad was *beguiled by the idea of his own death* and, when he had seen the Grail, he returned into his own land and said little of his adventure. When the other knights asked him where he had been, he would only say: 'I have been only where all of us will go one day.' "

He closed the book and, returning it to its shelf, looked up at me rather wearily, like some wise priest regarding at a wayward member of his flock who was his especial concern.

"I'm afraid, Edward. I'm afraid to go into his Sick Bay and be under his care. Can't you understand that? I'm afraid to fall into the clutches of Dr. Death."

"But there'll be Miss Daphne, too."

"Yes, that's true. Miss Daphne belongs in the game. She's a power certainly. Who is she, though?" He took out his set and began leafing through the cards, putting them down, one by one, face up. The Merchant, the Priest, the Hangman, the Soldier, the Judge, Pellinore, Galahad, Thor, Hod, Puck, Hermes, Christ, Merlin, Zoroaster, the King—where could we find Miss Daphne among this lot?

And yet I also felt that Miss Daphne belonged in the game, especially if the ground of the game was indeed, as Hadley had suggested, the school itself. I became lost in thought: perhaps Miss Daphne, as a woman, was outside of the game, perhaps she represented what was not included in the game. Like my mother. If everyone was in the game, how would we ever escape it?

Hadley had taken a piece of card and was drawing. He was an able draughtsman and under his fingers there began to emerge a woman, a woman with features neither pretty nor plain, with long, abundant hair, with full lips and high cheekbones and with a slender crown in her hand. Then he took his colours and coloured the hair auburn and the lips red putting a beauty spot high on her right cheek, adding some shade so that her face seemed to lengthen, and touching in her eyes with dark brown, and in the end she did look something like my mother, something like Miss Daphne, and something like a woman I had never met.

"It's the Queen," he said. "The missing card."

I had quite forgotten the Queen, the missing Queen, whose only existence until now, so far as I was concerned, had been in that jotted note of my father's dated ix.ix.55. How had I forgotten that all the time we had been playing with an incomplete pack? Surely the game had been impoverished by her absence. Imagine playing cards without Queens! Or chess!

It is curious how the eye sees what it wants to see, how it omits what does not concern it. I had read the instructions many times and, of course, there had been clauses regarding the movements of the Queen; but since there was no Queen in the pack, my eye had simply skated over these sentences, just as people drive over a zebra crossing when there's nobody using it.

But thanks to Hadley, there she was again.

"She's beautiful, Hadley," I said. "We'll reinstate her immediately."

I picked up the card and started to get out my game, but he protested.

"She belongs in my pack, I think," he said quietly.

This hadn't occurred to me, but I could scarcely deny the justice of it.

"Yes," I said. "You're right."

So he added the Queen to his pack.

"Let's play," he said.

We played, using his set, and it brought a new excitement to the proceedings because of the Queen, not knowing her powers, or when she would turn up. While Hadley laid the board out, I went and got the dice from my own set. "I prefer the old dice," I said, and Hadley raised no objection. He suggested we should go to the woods, but I felt suddenly confident that no one would bother us. The prospect of playing again, with Hadley, but in the warm and familiar surroundings of the sixth form, filled me with something like joy.

"Before we start," Hadley said, "I think I ought to remind you to be careful. Remember what we're playing for."

I didn't really care, but I trusted him.

"We're playing for the health of the whole school, Edward. We're playing against Death and against the Hangman. Pellinore is Avery and Miss Daphne's the Queen and you are Galahad and I…"

"Yes, go on. Who are you?" I was suddenly interested. "If I am Galahad, then who are you?"

"I'm Merlin, of course." He said it firmly, but with a faint air of embarrassment, as if he thought he might be claiming too much.

I looked at his Merlin card and laughed. Hadley blushed, but I wasn't laughing at him, only with him. He had drawn Merlin youthful and pale, earnest, withdrawn, like someone who is hiding his powers behind a shy countenance. Just like Hadley himself.

And I remembered, too, how in all our games, Hadley had favoured Merlin. Merlin and Pellinore, the shy giants.

I felt greatly comforted that Hadley was Merlin, and it occurred to me how in the Arthurian tales it was Merlin who had brought Galahad to the Round Table.

The game began.

CHAPTER EIGHT

MERLIN

I think that of all the games we played, this one, which took place in the corner of the sixth form on the eve of our struggle with the Doctor, was the most uncanny.

Hadley drew Merlin and I drew Galahad. I decided to make straight for the Dungeon and suggested that he should set off towards the Healing Stone, at all costs avoiding places where he might encounter Death, or the Doctor, as we now thought of him.

Galahad immediately got imprisoned in the maze, and some dismal throwing kept him trapped there. I needed a guide to get out, but I couldn't find one. Hadley reached the Healing Stone, where he drew Christ. Although he was in a strong position he seemed nervous and more than usually silent. He showed no inclination to leave the relative safety of the Healing Stone.

Eventually I got out of the maze and moved to the Dungeon where I drew the Hangman. I had not noticed Hadley's version of the Hangman card before and it gave me a jolt to see how accurately he had captured Tyson's features – and Tyson in one of his worst moods. The forehead and temples were coloured an angry red and the eyes were set in a threatening stare behind the thick lenses. My first instinct was to discard him, but Hadley pointed out that he might then turn up in a far more dangerous situation and that he was best kept under the watchful eye of Galahad in his fortress.

Both of us, of course, were on the lookout for the appearance of Death, and for a while we played a deliberate stand-off, both keeping our positions, but doing little or nothing to advance the situation.

Then I decided on a reckless move. After all, I had recently come face to face with the dreaded Doctor, and he had not frightened me then. I left the Dungeon and headed into the Fourth Kingdom, where, either at the Dole or Devilish, Death might certainly be found. Hadley started to protest at such a foolhardy scheme.

"Perhaps he won't show up at all," he said.

I pointed out to him that in that case we would have achieved nothing. The Doctor was the number one enemy and a game without him in it wouldn't help anybody. He had to agree to this, for it was he, and not I, who was to enter the Doctor's realm that very evening.

The plan worked beautifully. Galahad made it to the Dole and diced with Death. I threw a six; Hadley, for Death, a four.

Death's sting was drawn and he was turned face downward.

Hadley was jubilant. He even shook my hand. He felt better already, he said. But the game had to be played to a conclusion. Galahad moved to the Hermitage where he made an alliance with Pellinore. Hadley produced a series of unlucky throws and Merlin was forced to leave the Healing Stone. He landed on the Winds, and got blown straight into the Fourth Kingdom and onto the Dole. There, he could only play Merlin again by confronting Death, and so he chose to return to play Christ from the Healing Stone. But the dice didn't get any kinder and, in spite of all I could do to avoid him, he met the Hangman and was defeated. Merlin was his only remaining card. He had to play him.

The Death card was turned face up again and we threw. Four each. In the case of a draw with Death, the character is not actually killed, but he has to return to his place and the player loses the card. As Hadley possessed no other cards in his hand, the game was over.

All his cheerfulness evaporated at once. I tried to persuade him that there was no need for despair, reminding him that Death had been defeated by Galahad, and that Merlin had survived. Christ admittedly had been overcome, but we didn't even know who Christ represented.

"I think he just represents the power of goodness," he said. "Good was defeated by Tyson, that's what happened."

I had to admit to myself that this sounded plausible.

"We'll settle Tyson next time," I said.

Hadley could no longer postpone going into quarantine. He found that he had been allocated a bed in the annexe to the Sick Bay, which he took to be a sign that the game was already working itself out. When he left he was in a mood of deep depression even though I told him, promised him, that everything would be OK, and that he should just concentrate on getting well as quickly as possible, because I couldn't play without him and it might be necessary to play again soon.

The next morning there was more news. Other schools had been closed down, and I could see that Tyson had begun to view it as a point of honour that his school should stay open, and that we should not be allowed to give up 'like a bunch of weaklings,' as he expressed it at breakfast. There was a rumour at break that one of the boys from a neighbouring school had died from the 'flu. I never did find out whether this was true or not, but it certainly served to increase the tension at the time. The front pages of the newspapers began talking about 'this exceptionally virulent epidemic' and reported fatalities among the old and the weak. The weather turned bitterly cold and the sky was leaden. The pitches were too hard for football and the ranks of staff and pupils alike were so depleted as to make lessons a mere pretence of learning.

The following day only half the boys attended assembly and I heard Avery at lunch grumbling loudly at Tyson's insistence that the school should be kept open. It was just the sort of instance of Tyson's stubbornness best calculated to infuriate him.

Perhaps the disheartening news of all was that Miss Daphne herself was sick, which meant that fussy, bearded Miss Maber was left in charge of the sick rooms. It occurred to me for the first time that the Queen had not turned up in our game the day before, and now I understood why not. I imagined that the same thought would have occurred to poor Hadley.

Then, from one of the junior matrons I got actual news of him. He was not at all well, she told me. 'One of the worst cases. In fact, old Miss Maber told me…'–here she broke off, looking guiltily over my shoulder. Miss Maber herself had appeared, seemingly from nowhere.

"Yes, Miss Morrison," she said nastily, "and what did *old* Miss Maber tell you?" Not only did she have a beard, but in it there lurked a huge, unsightly wart. "Nothing, I hope, to do with the welfare of her patients, because in that case I'm sure *old* Miss Maber did not mean you to discuss it with every Tom, Dick and Harry in the school." Miss Morrison blushed and muttered an apology. Miss Maber waddled off, followed by a look of loathing from the pretty Miss Morrison. I felt sorry for her and frustrated that I didn't hear the end of the story.

Nor did I hear for a couple of days. The school continued its grim, embattled existence, Tyson more than ever determined not to give way, the rest of the staff enduring his determination with ill-concealed bad humour.

I was reading *The Arthurian Romances* at my desk when Tyson sent for me. Any summons to Tyson's study made me feel weak at the knees, and I don't suppose I was alone in this. Reluctantly I put down the book and went.

I knocked at the tall, oak-panelled door and heard a call of "Wait" from inside. I stood there wondering for what sort of people such huge doors were made. The handle was at the level of my neck.

After a while the door was opened, but not by Tyson. It was Doctor Fell. Tyson was sitting at his desk and when he spoke it was in a tone of suppressed fury.

"Now listen to me carefully," he said, "because I don't expect to have to repeat myself." He eyed me unsympathetically. "I must say I expected better of you, Yeoman. Here we are, going through the worst epidemic in my twenty years as Headmaster of this school, and it appears I must be bothered by childish pranks the like of which which I never thought to have to put up with within my own sixth form. Dr. Fell here,—who, I might add, is working round the clock for the health of your friends and fellow pupils—has come to me with the story of some game you've been playing. You and your friend Hadley."

I said nothing. I couldn't think what to reply, and anyway my vocal chords seemed to have seized up.

"So, you have no comment. Well, what if I were to tell you that John Hadley is at this moment seriously ill, and that as far as I can make out you are to blame?"

How much did he know and how had he found out? Above all, what could I say to throw him off the scent?

"I… I hope not, sir," I managed.

But he was simply waiting for my first words to unleash the full force of his anger.

"You hope not. I should damn well think you do hope not. I haven't got time now to go into this properly and decide on a fitting punishment for whatever you've been up to—there'll be the opportunity for that later. But I do know that if I don't have the whole story from you this minute, you'll have six of the best from me, six of the very best I can manage, right here and now. So let's hear from you."

"About what, sir?" I asked, and then, seeing the danger of an imminent explosion, I went on. "The game's nothing, really sir, nothing at all. It's just a game."

Tyson's frame trembled as he sought to contain his anger. I had often seen him like this, with Tom and others, but this was the first time I had been the victim of one of his rages. He looked towards his cane cupboard, as if selecting a weapon.

"How do you explain, then, Yeoman, the good Doctor's story?" Here he gestured towards the Doctor who was standing behind me, out of my sight. "I understand that Hadley has been raving in his fevered sleep, raving repeatedly about some game, about a somebody or something called Doctor Death, and about *you*, Yeoman."

Again I said nothing. Nothing came.

"Perhaps you don't believe me? Perhaps you'd like to hear it from the Doctor himself?"

I shook my head, meaning that I did believe him, but Tyson was in a mood to interpret things however it suited him.

"You don't believe me, eh? Well, we'll see about all this later. Meanwhile, Doctor, would you care to oblige us with your story."

I half-turned to where the Doctor was standing. In front, the Hangman. Behind, Death.

The Doctor was smooth, silky.

"Yes, yes. Well, I don't suppose it's anything that can't be cleared up in a trice," he said. "The boy Hadley is gravely ill." I didn't like that word gravely. "And he seems to be worrying himself unduly about this game, so I felt it would be a good idea if you could help us sort out the problem. He's mentioned your name several times. 'Where's Yeoman?' he cried out to me once. 'Where's Yeoman to fight with Death?'"

"What exactly did he mean by that, Yeoman?" Tyson hissed.

By this point my mind had started working again, and I realised that neither Tyson nor the doctor knew very much. Yet I obviously had to give them some kind of explanation.

"It's as I said, sir, it's only a game that we play. But Hadley takes it rather seriously, and I suppose that some of the characters are a bit frightening. And now with his illness…"

I wondered if that would be enough. It wasn't.

"Well, let's just have a little look at this game of yours, Yeoman, and we'll hear the rest of what you've got to say with the proper evidence in front of us."

"Yes, sir, I'll go and get it." I turned to go, almost with relief. I already knew what I would do. I would give him Hadley's set. Without the instructions the game would mean virtually nothing. It would just look like any old game.

"Wait," said Tyson. "I'll come with you, just to see there's no doctoring of the evidence." He turned to Doctor Fell with a mirthless smile. "No offence to you, Doctor. Now, where do you keep it?" he added to me shortly as we left the room.

"In the sixth form, sir. It's in Hadley's desk."

But as we proceeded down the corridor, a ghastly thought occurred to me. Hadley's Hangman card—nobody could mistake whom it portrayed. If Tyson saw the Hangman card, that would be enough. He would need to see no more. Such a ruthless caricature of himself would amount to treason, high treason. In my own game the card was not so recognisable—or at least it wouldn't be to him—but my game contained the instructions and my father's letter, and all would be revealed. Besides, I wasn't going to give my game away, not without a struggle.

I had one slim chance.

We entered the sixth form. There were a couple of boys there.

"Leave us," said Tyson peremptorily.

One of the boys was Abbott, reading as usual. He was a real slowcoach, Abbott: he took his time over whatever he did.

I reached Abbott's desk.

"Leave us, I said," yelled Tyson.

Abbott carefully inserted his bookmark. I opened Hadley's desk. There was the package. Scarcely daring to breathe, I pulled the game out of its wrapping, opened the box, slid my hand in, and felt for the cards. Then I removed the very top card and slipped it among the other things at the bottom of the desk. I closed the box and drew it out just as Tyson arrived at my side. Abbott had finally left the room, closing the door behind him.

"All of it," said Tyson, "I want all of it."

"That's just the wrapper, sir," I said.

He picked it up, shook it, looked inside and threw it down.

"All right, give me the box and follow me back to my study"

And we were out in the corridor again. I prayed for luck. It so happened that one of my trivial superstitions regarding the game was to return the cards to the pack, at the end of play, with the winning or dominant card at the very top. The Hangman had won the previous game by his defeat of Christ. Had I followed my usual habit? I couldn't remember.

Back in Tyson's study the game was deposited on the desk and opened. The Doctor seemed particularly eager to inspect the contents. I wondered if he knew more about it than he had told Tyson.

The board was laid out and the cards examined. I tried to tell by Tyson's expression whether the offending card was still in the pack. He looked through them one by one, keeping a single card aside, and, when he had inspected them all, he threw that card down on the desk. It was Death.

I took a long breath. If the Hangman had been there, I should have known about it by now.

"This is the famous Doctor Death, I presume," said Tyson.

"Yes, sir."

Hadley's drawing of the Death card, although as long and cadaverous as the original, bore no special resemblance to Dr. Fell.

"And why *Doctor* Death, might I ask?" said the Doctor.

"That's just our name for him, sir," I said. "No particular reason."

"I see," he said, giving me a quizzical look.

Tyson was examining the board.

"How's this damn thing played?" he said. "Where are the instructions anyway?"

"Well, sir, you see, the game was invented by Hadley and me, completely homemade, as it were. So we've been sort of working out the play as we go along. Nothing's been written down, it's all in our heads."

"And what's your explanation for Hadley's obsession?" asked Tyson, in a somewhat friendlier tone. I knew well enough what was happening. Tyson's sense of values was being confirmed for him. It would suit him much better to assume that Hadley was over-reacting in a typically neurotic fashion, than that Edward Yeoman, son of a World War Two pilot, good cricketer, cheerful and personable young man, was exercising a sinister influence.

I played up to him, as I always did.

"Well, I think, sir, if you'll forgive me saying so, that Hadley had made the game rather important to him, and when he kept losing…"

"Ah, he kept losing, did he?"

"Yes, sir."

"And it became rather an obsession with him. That's it, isn't it?"

"Something like that, sir."

"Well I must say the game looks harmless enough, don't you think so, Doctor?"

"On the surface, yes. I must admit that it does." He was again looking at me rather curiously.

This wasn't wholehearted support, but Tyson was one of those people who, when his mind is firmly made up, simply ignores all other possibilities.

"Even so," said Tyson, "there's no question of the game being returned to you. This fascination with death must not be encouraged, and clearly some aspect of the game must have worried Hadley. So I think the best place for it…" Here he stuffed the various pieces of the game into its box, picked it up and began opening the doors of the old stove that heated the room. He would certainly have consigned it to the flames, had Dr. Fell not made a surprisingly abrupt move to restrain him.

"If you'll allow me, Headmaster," he said, taking the game from his hands, "I'd be interested to keep this in my possession for a while. If young Hadley continues to rave about it I may be able to work out what has disturbed him and thereby find the appropriate remedy. He is quite lucid when his temperature is down in the mornings, and I may be able to use this to get some sense out of him. A feverish coma is not itself unexpected with such high temperatures, but these frantic anxieties are certainly worrying and we must see what we can do about them."

This speech was delivered in a particularly 'doctorish' tone, no doubt to forestall any possibility of Tyson's disagreeing. In this he had gauged his man correctly, for Tyson was always one to defer to the opinions of professional men. Lawyers and Doctors, I think, ranked next to noblemen and war heroes in his personal hierarchy.

"Very well, Doctor, as you wish. Yeoman, you may leave us now and I hope that we can consider the matter closed."

"Yes sir. Thank you sir. I'm sorry if I've caused any trouble sir."

Tyson chuckled and laid his hand on my head. *In loco parentis.*

"You're a good boy, Yeoman, a good boy."

"Sir, I wonder if I might be allowed to see Hadley. We're good friends and I might be able to reassure him. About the game, I mean."

"That sounds like a reasonable idea. What do you think, Doctor?"

"No. I don't think we should break our careful rules about quarantine, Headmaster. And I fear that Hadley could find a visit from his young friend at this point more upsetting than otherwise."

"Whatever you say, Doctor." Tyson replied, though he seemed puzzled at this objection. I was less puzzled. I was beginning to get some ideas about Dr. Fell.

It wasn't until that night, as I lay in bed, that I had a chance to think over the afternoon's work. I had meanwhile retrieved the Hangman card from the bottom of Hadley's desk and added it to my own set. Then I wrapped the game in a plastic bag, and finding I had ten minutes to spare before the bell for tea, I ran with my parcel to the woods and buried it among the pine needles of our disused camp. I thought of Tom and missed him with a pang that took me by surprise.

That night I applied my mind to the problem of Doctor Fell. I felt sure that he had learnt more from Hadley than he had told Tyson, and that his real reason for getting hold of the game was not to aid Hadley's recovery but to satisfy some curiosity of his own, a curiosity that I instinctively mistrusted. He had obviously not believed me when I had said that the name Doctor Death held no significance. Nor had he appeared convinced by my explanation for the lack of instructions.

What exactly was his interest?

I also gave some thought to our last game. Its most striking aspect had been Galahad's defeat of Death. All the rest seemed to be working out according to pattern. Merlin was seriously ill, in Death's clutches. Tyson, the Hangman, was in control. He had even, in a sense, become my ally in believing my story and supporting my version of the facts. Everything fitted apart from Galahad's feat.

It was late at night and I still couldn't sleep. There was complete silence from downstairs, and I could tell by the absence of reflected light on the terrace below our dormitory that the lights in the library and Tyson's study were out. I decided on a bold plan. I would go and see Hadley in the Sick Bay and warn him of what was going on.

Looking back on it I can see it was a crazy scheme but I was at that time so caught up in the spirit of the game, that I conceived of myself not as a boy trespassing dangerously in the corridors of a sleeping school, but as Galahad moving fearlessly from his castle to the Dole, where, I was certain, he was assured of success. All the same, I prepared an alibi. If discovered I would claim that I had been very sick and was looking for the matron. Given the epidemic, it seemed as likely a tale as any.

I had a small pencil torch which I used for reading under the blankets after lights out. I put on dressing gown and slippers and set off, keeping the torch for emergencies.

It was a hell of a long way from my dormitory to the Sick Bay, from one end of the whole school to the other. Not counting two flights of stairs, the changing rooms and the huge cavernous gym — which at night, without a light, felt something like a sleeping railway station — there must have been a furlong of corridors.

Those corridors. I have more memories located in the corridors of that school than in any single room. The corridors were the true common land. The rules said no running in corridors, no shouting, no games, but these injunctions were freely and perpetually ignored. The corridors belonged to the boys and there was nothing that anybody else could do about it. I remember games of marbles, games with toy soldiers, games of catch and games of tag. I remember furtive meetings, exchanges of secret gifts and of course, those long, nervous journeys to Tyson's study ending in long, nervous waits outside his door.

But my journey that night was the longest and most nervous of all. I found that I dared not switch on my torch for fear of discovery. Some stretches were blacker than black. I felt my way along the walls, trying to gauge the intervals between the doors so as not to stumble accidentally into one of the dormitories or, worse still, into the bedroom of a teacher or matron.

Usually there were dim, ghostly lamps lit in the corridor of the junior wing, but perhaps the grim Miss Maber had had them turned off for the sake of economy. She had none of Miss Daphne's concern for the night-time fears of little boys.

But at last I came to the annexe. Under the door was a thin line of light. I put my ear to the panel. Silence. I turned the door handle gently and pushed. There was only one bed inside, as I had remembered. In it I could make out the sleeping form of John Hadley. I bent to wake him.

"Come in, young Yeoman, come in."

In the corner, propped up in an easy chair, sat Dr. Fell.

"Don't just stand there letting the cold in. Come in."

He was right. It was freezing. I had no choice but to go in, closing the door behind me.

"Come on," he said again cheerily. "There's a spare chair here, next to me."

He was sitting on the far side of the bed, near to the light. In his hand was a pencil and a writing pad. I saw with a shock that he had the game, Hadley's game, laid out on a small folding table beside him.

"Yes, the game, the game," he said with a sigh, watching me carefully. He motioned me to the chair beside him. I circled the bed and sat down. For a moment I had considered making my escape at the double, but what good would that have done? Whatever trouble I was in, I was already in it.

"I hoped you might come," he said. "In fact I was expecting you. I think that your visit could save me a lot of time. The truth is that I'm having trouble with this game of yours. Without the instructions, that is," he said with meaning.

I said nothing.

"Yes, of course, I understand your reticence. Must have been a bit of a shock for the young Galahad, mustn't it? Look, how about a cup of cocoa? I'm well prepared for an all-night vigil, and I have here …" he bent to pick up something beside him "… a flask of hot cocoa and some biscuits. Even a banana if you'd care for one. No? Well, have some cocoa anyway."

As he poured me a cup, I wondered about that reference to Galahad. Either he already knew a great deal or it was a very lucky shot.

I took the cocoa. He rose and turned up the little gas fire in the corner. I began to feel a bit more comfortable, although his face was disquieting in the feeble light which had the effect of emphasising the steep cragginess of his brow and the long hollow cheeks.

"There, that's a little better, isn't it? Now, let me assure you, you've got nothing to worry about where this nocturnal expedition of yours is concerned. I won't tell a soul. In fact I'll do better than that. If you're discovered here, or on your way back, you can say that I fetched you to be with your friend Hadley, that he was asking for you. Mr. Tyson will quite understand, won't he? I'm a law unto myself here at the moment, for who would interfere with the good Doctor giving up his night's sleep to sit with a patient in danger. Who indeed?" He laughed unpleasantly. "Oh, as for Hadley, you can stop worrying. He's getting better. His temperature's much lower tonight and he's sleeping well. In the morning, I fancy, he'll be more like his normal self."

He paused. "That's part of the trouble, you see. He's stopped giving me information about the game. That's why your arriving like this is such a godsend, for now…" He leant toward me and lowered his voice to a whisper, "Now you'll be able to tell me all about it."

I had still said nothing. My mind was working furiously, but no plan came to save me. I couldn't tell him the truth, but I had to satisfy him somehow and he didn't seem an easy man to fool. I decided to stall, hoping to discover what he already knew and how much I would have to tell him.

"Well, I'd like to help you of course, sir, but I'm a bit confused. I mean, what is it that you want to know?"

He laughed again, but there was no more humour in it than before.

"To begin with," he said, "I know that this game here is not the original." I suppose I should have denied this at once, but I hesitated, and then it was too late. Correctly, he took my silence as confirmation. "Good. Next, I know that you are Galahad, that poor Hadley is Merlin and I've a good idea of who I am."

I still couldn't make the necessary disavowals. I would have to hear him out in silence.

"Then there's the crucial point. What are the powers of the game? And what…" His eyes narrowed and his voice dropped. "…what is the origin of those powers?" He was quiet for a while before continuing. "The game is old. That is certain. Very, very old." He shot me a keen glance, as if expecting me to say something.

"A hundred years old?" I suggested at last.

"A hundred?" he said scornfully. "Thousands, more like. A relic from another age, this game of yours."

"But…but it couldn't be that old. It could never have survived…"

"No, no. I don't mean in this form. It will have changed its form many times, and will no doubt change again. It is the power that is ancient, more ancient than you can possibly imagine." He glared at me, frowning. "*Albion's Dream*, it's called, but it is more than a dream, Yeoman, much more than a dream. Albion's vision would be nearer the mark, and yet it still wouldn't describe it, because any seer may have a vision, but there are few who can impress the power of their vision on reality itself."

I could see that he was gripped by this idea. I imagined an ancient mystery, but I did not quite follow his words.

"How did the game come into your possession?" he asked suddenly.

"I found it."

"Ah." It sounded as if that was what he had expected. "Where?"

"Behind a bookshelf."

"Yes! It had been lost and then it was found. That is the way of such things. It was you that found it, but it was to me that it was destined to come."

Again he was silent and again he gave that peculiar chuckle, the sound of a man pleased at his own cleverness, a man not in the least vulnerable to the true, ordinary humour that real people laugh with. One of the least funny people I have ever met.

He turned to me suddenly, with the light of a new idea in his eyes.

"Listen. I heard of this game nearly twenty years ago. I heard of it in a small village in Somerset, by the name of Turnworth."

This time I couldn't conceal my amazement. I actually couldn't believe my ears.

"Turnworth? What do you know of Turnworth?"

"Quite a lot, I should say. I was born only three miles from there. I was at school with your Uncle Jack. He was a good lad, Jack, although for some reason he never really liked me. I can't think why, I never did anything to harm him. Anyway, the time I'm thinking of was the winter of 1932 or '33, Christmastime it must have been. I was walking down the lane through Turnworth, on the way to the 'Swan' for a lunchtime drink, I expect, when I met Jack, or rather he hurtled into me, coming from the garden of your family house. He was extremely upset. I'd never seen him so agitated. He had tears running down his cheeks. I caught hold of him and tried to calm him down, and eventually got him to sit on a large stone by the side of the road. He was scarcely intelligible, but he kept on saying something about a blasted game, an unholy game – a witches' game, he called it.

"'I lost her because of the game,' he said. 'She was mine and the game took her from me.' I could get no more out of him than this, but as you can imagine it stuck in my mind as such – shall I say *occult*? – fragments do, and later I heard independently that his elder brother had taken his girl and I put the two bits of information together.

"I once got a bit drunk with Jack, a couple of years later and I asked him about it, but he wouldn't tell me a thing. Simply changed the subject. I'd completely forgotten about it in fact until two days ago when young Hadley started mumbling. Curiously enough he used almost the same words. 'The damned game. I'm alone because of the game. I can't get out of the game and the Doctor will get me.' And so on. And then there was the strange coincidence of your being at the school. You had brought yourself to my attention by your strange behaviour at the window and when the matron told me your name I saw the family resemblance and guessed who you were. Then Hadley mentioned you in his ramblings and things began to fit together. And now here I am with the game and no instructions. But instead of the instructions I've got you, haven't I?"

He was very sinister when he said this. But his story had at least given me the hint of a plan. I decided to try it at once, while I still had the nerve.

"You see, Dr. Fell, the instructions are lost."

"What?" He half-rose from his chair.

"Yes," I went on quickly. "I found the game but there were no instructions. I asked Jack, but he just wanted to take the game from me. He thought it had been destroyed, you see, and he was pleased when he heard that the instructions were lost. He wanted me never to mention it to my father and I never did."

"Then your father must have them. You must get them from your father."

The way he said it, it sounded like an order.

I hurried on. "So we had to work it out, Hadley and I, and, well, we just made a mess of it. I knew, from Jack's reaction as much as anything, that there was some secret about it, and I told Hadley so, and then it's true that some odd things began to happen and we got a bit frightened and decided to stop playing and…"

He cut me short.

"But where is the original?"

"Oh that. That's at home. I didn't like to have it at school. Hadley made the copy and we played with that."

"I want to see the original." Again that air of command – but although I was frightened of him, I began to realise that his hold over me was not as complete as he might have thought. After all, I knew as many of his secrets as he knew of mine if not more, but still I had to be careful. Mainly I had to get out of that dreadful little room with its dreadful, sickly light, its smell of illness and that cadaverous face.

He must have seen that he was pushing me too hard, because he changed his approach. He sat back in his chair and smiled his mirthless smile.

"So we both have the same problem, little Yeoman, don't we?

We both want to know how the game is really played, don't we? So we must cooperate. We must work out a plan how to get the instructions from your father. Now, if your father knew how badly you needed them…" He fell silent, thinking. "I think the first thing for me to do is to diagnose you unwell and consign you to the sick room. That way we'll be able to keep in close contact, won't we? Then we must compose a letter to your father. Yes, that's the way, we'll write to your father. But we must think of a bait, an irresistible bait." He looked at me as if measuring me up, as if deciding what sort of hook he would impale me on.

"Before we start putting our plan into action, however, there are a couple of details I'd be glad to know. Firstly, how did you come to cast me in the role of Death?"

"Oh that's easy. You just looked like the card in the original game."

"I did, did I?" Even he seemed vaguely uncomfortable at this information.

"Well, slightly, anyway. And then there was the epidemic, of course, and it just seemed to fit. I'm sorry," I went on. "It was stupid of us."

"Perhaps. The next question is: when did you last play the game?"

"We tried it a few days ago, but when you don't know the rules you get into all kinds of confusion and we couldn't make it work at all. So we left it."

He looked as if he didn't believe me.

MERLIN

"Hadley's been very feverish, hasn't he Doctor? I don't expect he's been making much sense. He's got a terrific imagination, really he has. He used to spin all these amazing stories, and the game just became part of his stories. It was really he who thought of Doctor Death and told me I was Galahad and he was Merlin. I thought it was all a bit crazy if you want to know. Exciting of course, but crazy. Now with what you've told me I can see that he was right in a way, but personally I always thought it was just a game."

He wasn't quite convinced. I got out my handkerchief and managed a bit of a sniffle, catching my breath as if holding back a sob. I'm not a bad actor when pushed to it and I was scared, properly scared.

"To tell the truth, I'm a bit frightened by it all. I'll try and help you get the instructions, if there are any, although Jack was sure they must have been destroyed—but I don't want any more to do with it. I'll get them for you if I can, but I'd just like to forget the whole thing." I blew my nose loudly.

"Yes yes. Quite. It must be upsetting for you." He even laid a hand on my shoulder. I suppose the gesture was meant to comfort me, but it felt cold and menacing.

"Now we'll have to convince old Miss M and the rest that you really are ill. We can't have then sending you off as a malingerer, can we?" He got up and moved to the corner of the room where I could see his bag. I knew then that I had to be ready to move. The word game was played out. I stood up as if to prepare myself for treatment.

"I think this should do the trick," he said, and as he straightened up I saw a hypodermic syringe in his hand and the glint of a needle. I was like a little pig who suddenly gets the idea that the knife is for him. I was far too quick for him, off-guard as he was. I was over the bed and out of the door before he'd even moved, and I didn't make the mistake of going back the way I'd come, either. Just outside the annexe door was a staircase descending to the lower classrooms. I threw myself at the stairwell, half- fell, half-stumbled down the steps, bruised but in one piece, at the bottom. From there it was a few steps to the practice piano and the bow window by White Cliffs. I was out of the window before I even heard the Doctor's step on the stairs. He dared not shout, I suppose, and he had no idea of the geography of the place.

I didn't feel safe to return to my own bed. I wanted a lot more secure than that. It was freezing cold, and I was clad only in pyjamas and dressing gown. I considered the cricket pavilion, but no doubt it would be locked and, perhaps, hardly warmer than it was outside. I thought of Tom's camp. Hopeless.

I couldn't face going back into the main building. I imagined Dr. Fell's awful face at every window and every door. I saw again the syringe and the needle. Who knows what he would load it with next time? For a while I thought that there was nowhere to go. But I remembered the sequence of the game and Pellinore's Hermitage.

CHAPTER NINE

GALAHAD

TO reach Avery's home I had to cross the road. I felt pretty odd doing this after midnight in my nightclothes, and it would have been awkward for me if I had been spotted. But the desire to put distance between me and the Doctor was stronger than any other fear, and there was not a soul in sight as I slipped over the road and through the big wooden gates that led to the senior football pitch. I crossed the pitch by the goalposts and made my way through the Avery's rose garden to the door of their little house. I scarcely hesitated before ringing the bell, keeping the button pressed as long as I dared.

A light went on and I heard the sound of footsteps. The door opened and there was Fred Avery. Somehow it struck me as funny seeing him in his pyjamas. I'd never seen him in anything but his shapeless red-brown sports jacket and perhaps I'd assumed he slept in it as well.

"Good Lord, Yeoman. What the devil?"

For a moment he looked annoyed, but he must have sensed that this was no schoolboy prank and he pulled me in and shut the door. At the touch of his hand on my arm, I collapsed against him and he caught me to stop me from falling. "Eileen. EILEEN," he called. "Come down here a moment, will you?"

He pushed me into one of the rooms, turned on the light and sat me in a chair. Then, bending over the fireplace, he began to blow a little light into the dying embers of the fire. "Good Lord, boy, you must be freezing." He looked about and found a rug, which he draped over my shoulders. I was shivering uncontrollably. As he went to add some kindling to the flame, his wife came in. I hardly knew her, but she recognised me quickly enough.

"Yeoman, isn't it? Well well, what a time for a visit." She came close to me. "Why, you're trembling, poor boy. Here, let me rub a little warmth into you." And she began to rub my shoulders and back soothingly. I can tell you it was a delicious sensation. "Pour him a brandy, Alfred. I think he needs it." Mr. Avery brought me a small glass of brandy, and at the same moment the fire caught hold of the twigs and flared up. Quite suddenly I felt much better.

It reminded me of home, this wonderful, *normal* place with the tidy chairs and sofa, the lamps, the fender, the tongs, the tray with two cups of some late night beverage, and the marvellous warmth of the fire, the brandy, and Mrs. Avery's hands.

Avery had sat down opposite me and was looking at me out of the corner of his eye.

"Now explain yourself, Yeoman," he said. "And it had better be good to justify getting us out of bed at this time of night." He never really smiled, Avery, the corners of his mouth just quivered a little when he was pleased with something.

"It's rather a long story, sir," I said.

"Well, now we're up, we can stay up for a while," said Avery. "Put on a cup of tea, will you, Eileen?"

"I will," she said brightly. "But don't start the story yet. I don't want to miss anything."

I lay back in my chair, and Mr. Avery added some logs to the fire. I felt deeply content. Then I sat up.

"Is the door locked, sir?"

"Yes, it is." Again there was his ghost of a smile. "Is someone going to attack us?"

"No, no, I don't think so." But he must have realised that something serious was worrying me, because he made a little show of getting up and going out to check the front door. I heard him rattling the lock. Actually I think he went to say something to his wife, too, because they returned together a few minutes later, he with the tea and she with a plate of biscuits.

"Now, out with it," Fred Avery said.

I thought I'd better start at the end, with the Doctor. I told them I'd been, against the rules, to visit Hadley in the sick room and that I'd met the Doctor there. I told them that he had become angry with me and threatened me with a hypodermic syringe. I could see Avery looking rather doubtful at this, but to my surprise Mrs. Avery came to my aid.

"I've never liked that man, Alfred," she said.

"He looks all right to me," he said. "Competent sort of bloke I thought. Better than the last one anyway."

"He may be a good doctor, but he is not a good man," said his wife firmly. "Now, go on with the story, Edward."

So then I went back a bit and explained about the game and about the events of the afternoon, about Hadley's coma and this idea of the Doctor's that there was some occult secret attached to the game. You see, I knew Fred quite well in a way. I had been taught by him for five years and I knew him in the special way that a pupil can know a teacher — from a distance, of course, and in ignorance of nearly all the intimate details of his daily and domestic life, like the business of his pyjamas, but still with some true understanding of the quality of his spirit and of the deeper inclinations of his mind. I knew, for example, that he was no lover of the metaphysical, that he would be impatient of things that I remember him referring to as 'muck and mystery'. What I needed was to persuade him that Dr. Fell was a dangerous man and that my flight from him was not caused by the wild imaginings of a child, but was the result of getting on the wrong side of a lunatic. I saw that I had caught Fred's interest, but it wasn't until he spoke to his wife that I realised why.

"If he's right about this man, Eileen, you know what it could mean."

"Of course I do. And he is right. Look at the poor boy. Do you really think he'd come over here in the freezing cold at one o'clock in the morning to tell us a tall story?" She poured me some more tea.

"No. Now, if the Doctor is nuts, which seems likely, and if Tyson is nuts, which is certain –" here he shot me a sly glance which I understood at once as a pledge of secrecy – "then we can stop this business here and now." I assumed he was referring to Tyson's decision not to close the school, but perhaps he had something more radical in mind.

"Which means, Yeoman, that you'd better keep out of sight for a while."

"Alfred, we can hardly *hide* him. They'd take a very dim view of that."

I was happy to go along with whatever they suggested, but I knew more than they did, and I had to make sure of certain things. I had to see Hadley, without confronting the Doctor. Also I wanted to get at my package under the pine needles. And I was sure that my best camouflage would be provided by the normal routine of school.

"I think I'd better go back, sir," I said.

"Yes, I suppose you had."

"But not now please, sir."

"No, no. Not now, of course," said Mrs. Avery. She turned to her husband. "But what about the Doctor? Supposing he tries some other awful business tomorrow?" She shuddered. "What a terrible man. You must have been frightened out of your wits. my dear. But I don't quite understand why he wanted to make you ill."

She was very nice, Mrs. Avery, and very friendly, but she was quite acute, too, and obviously she wanted to be sure of my story. So I told them again of the Doctor's obsession with this game of ours and how he wanted some information from me about it, information I didn't even have. I repeated my account of how he had threatened me in the half-light of the little annexe. It was not hard for me to tell it vividly, and I knew that they believed me.

"I think you'll be safe enough during the day," said Avery. "When it comes to tomorrow night, we'll think again. It should be easy for you to slip over here with me. The school's in such a mess at the moment that I don't suppose anyone will notice."

I agreed to this scheme, although I had my own idea of dealing with the Doctor that I kept to myself.

I didn't sleep well that night. Even with the clean sheets and the warm blankets and a night light that Mrs. Avery left for me.

"You call out if you need anything," she told me. "I'm a light sleeper and I'm only next door."

But the little room and the single bed and the night light reminded me too sharply of another little room and another little light and of an encounter that had shaken Sir Galahad to the core.

In the morning Mrs. Avery found me a school uniform from somewhere and Mr. Avery took me back to school. We went through the gate that led in behind the kitchens and I joined the rest of the boys as they filed into breakfast. Some of my friends had noticed my absence early that morning, but so far as I could learn none of the staff had seen or commented on it.

As soon as I got the chance, I sat down and wrote a letter to my father. I kept it short and simple, telling him that I had come across an old game of his – I gave a brief description – and that the rules were missing, and asking him if he knew of their whereabouts. If so would he be kind enough to forward them to me, as the game looked interesting and I thought it might be fun to play? I finished the letter with a couple of snippets of ordinary news, signed it and put it in an envelope.

During break, having first checked that the little red car was not in the car park, I went off to look for Miss Morrison and discovered when the Doctor was expected for his morning round. I hoped to keep the initiative and did not want the Doctor to find me before I found him. Miss Morrison told me the Doctor didn't usually arrive until mid-day after his own surgery was over.

The best thing, I thought, was to turn up at the dispensary door before lunch, on the pretext of feeling unwell. I knew that I would not be alone, for each day still saw new victims of the 'alien virus'. There would be safety in numbers and the Doctor would be sure to have one of the matrons in attendance.

And so it proved. There were three or four boys already waiting when I arrived. Not wanting to be the last in the queue, I managed to persuade a couple of the boys to let me in before them. When I entered the dispensary, there was Dr. Fell, and with him the ancient, bearded matron. The Doctor looked up and his eyes narrowed unpleasantly. The next moment he recovered himself, but I could see that I had surprised him. I felt quite calm and collected;

it seemed that an age had passed since the nightmare of the previous evening.

"Excuse me, Dr. Fell, for using your valuable time, but I knew that you would want to see this." And I gave him the letter.

He looked quickly at the address.

"Thankyou," he said, putting it carefully in the pocket of his white coat. He seemed pleased. "I'm glad you found the time to write it."

"I thought if there was anything in it you wanted to discuss with me, I could come back at the end of your surgery. Would that be convenient?"

Again he showed pleasure at my suggestion. He clearly thought that my complicity in his designs was assured. This was as I had hoped.

"Yes," he said cheerfully. "That'll be fine." He looked at his watch. "About one o'clock, shall we say?"

When I left the room, another couple of boys had joined the queue, so that there were now five or six outside. Perfect. The door to the annexe was exactly opposite. I waited until the next boy had entered the dispensary, then I simply opened the door of the annexe and walked in.

Hadley was sitting up in bed, reading. He nearly yelled out on seeing me, but I motioned him to keep quiet and went up to the bed.

"How are you feeling, Hadley?" I whispered.

"OK. Much better today. But what are you doing here?"

"Listen. I've got to be quick."

And I told him, as briefly as I could, what had been going on. I didn't explain to him how they'd managed to find out about the game, but I got him to understand what to say to Dr. Fell or Tyson if they should question him.

I had nearly finished when the door opened. I spun round. It was Miss Morrison.

"Yeoman," she began accusingly, but I put my finger to my lips.

"Shh! Old Miss M," I whispered and gestured towards the dispensary.

She smiled, put her own finger to her lips, and withdrew.

Hadley wanted me to go into details but I didn't have time.

"Have you got the story?" I said.

"Yes, I think so."

"We never had the instructions, we never knew how to play the game properly and -" I paused, "- most important of all, you've got to get well at once. Even if you don't feel well."

"Why?"

"Because we've got to play the game again, dope."

And I left.

I was so sure of myself now, so pleased with myself, that I decided not to go back to class. In spite of Tyson's severe admonitions, in spite of his lists and arrangements and his unyielding insistence on discipline, the school was, as Avery had said, in a mess. Two more of the staff had gone down with the bug and there was a knot of boys outside one of the junior classrooms, while the noise from another told that there was no teacher inside.

Following my route of the night before, I climbed out of the window by the White Cliffs, circled the big playing fields, and reached the woods. My package was where I had left it. I removed the instructions and stowed the game back in its hiding place. Then I returned to the school buildings and chose a roundabout path to the sixth form.

There was a master at the desk but he showed no interest in my excuses. I had been to see the Doctor, I said.

"So what," he said. "So has everybody else." And he returned to his novel.

I sat down and wrote my letter to Mr. Hodman. After reminding him of our meeting on Dungeon Hill, I told him what had happened since, leaving out nothing of importance, and asked him to keep the enclosed documents safe for me until I could pick them up. I tried to think of a suitable way of ending the letter, of making him understand how serious I was. His own words came back to me. 'It's better to believe things,' I wrote, and put it in inverted commas. 'Please don't let me down,' I added as an afterthought.

I put this letter together with the instructions of the game in an envelope, sealed it, stamped it, and hid it carefully between two pages of *The Arthurian Romances*. The so-called lesson ended at one, and I went for my rendezvous with the Doctor.

He was waiting for me. The queue of boys had gone and so had

Miss Maber. I suppose I should have felt nervous at being alone with him, but I knew that nothing could go wrong. I remembered, you see, that Galahad had challenged Death and left him powerless.

"I read the letter," he said. "Just the job, I should think." He took it from his pocket. "Shall I post it for you?"

"Yes," I said, "the sooner the better."

"Fine. I'll pop it in the box this afternoon. Then all we have to do is wait."

He couldn't really have imagined that he would obtain the instructions so easily, but he apparently did believe that I was willing to help him. I thought I might be able to slip away at this point, but he had more to say.

"Now, young man, what about the other part of our agreement?" he said. "And what about your extraordinary behaviour last night? That wasn't how we'd planned it, was it? You should thank your lucky stars that I decided not to report you to your Headmaster this morning. I kept my side of the bargain even though you'd broken yours."

I knew he was bluffing, and I had my reply prepared, but the situation required caution. The needle, I knew, would still be in the bag, and we seemed to be pretty much on our own.

"I must apologise for that, Dr. Fell. It's just that I'm terrified of injections and probably I was tired and upset, and well…I just ran without thinking."

He was silent, calculating.

"And the other thing was," I went on, "I know it's stupid, but in the game, you see, you were…"

He laughed that laugh of his. "Oh yes, I was Doctor Death, wasn't I? Yes, I can see that might have worried you. I should have thought of that. But you understand now, don't you, that I'm no more Doctor Death than you are Sir Galahad?"

"Of course I understand now, sir, but at the time I suppose I just panicked."

"Right you are. Anyway, I think we can do without that particular complication now, can't we? The letter will be on its way this afternoon and – yes, what about the original version of the game?"

"I could bring it after half-term if you like, sir," I said. I played the role of penitent child for all it was worth.

"Yes," he said. "Do that thing."

"How is Hadley this morning, sir?"

"I've just seen Hadley and he's a great deal better, perfectly lucid. Temperature normal. And I must say that his version of events tallies pretty closely with your own. I didn't tell him of our little agreement. No doubt you'll let him know about that later, when he's back in circulation."

"When will that be, do you think, sir?"

"Oh not for a couple of days. He's still weak, naturally."

"And the game, Hadley's game. Will you be able to let us have it back?"

"No no. I don't think that would be right, would it? I mean it wouldn't be very fair to your Headmaster for a start. And then, I have certain experiments of my own to make."

This didn't worry me very much, for I knew he wouldn't get far without the rules. The main thing was that I had set his mind at ease by giving him the impression that with the letter and Hadley's game in his possession, he was calling the tune, whereas in fact I knew that both were worthless. The game without the instructions was nothing, and as for the the letter, well, not only did my father not have the instructions, but he was abroad on business for a fortnight and if all went as planned I would get my hands on the letter when I returned home at half-term, before my father had even seen it.

So I left Dr. Fell in the brightest of spirits. I had only one more task to perform, which was to send the letter to Mr. Hodman. I didn't want to put it in the school post, because Tyson did not allow letters to be sealed before he had the opportunity of examining them, and there was every chance that a missive from me to some unrelated gentleman in Dorset would arouse his curiosity. So I had decided to entrust it to Miss Morrison, who I knew would be happy to do me a favour without any questions asked. Besides, I looked forward to seeking her out in her little room opposite Keeper's Cottage. There had been rumours about Miss Morrison that I found rather exciting.

This last business would have to wait until after lunch. For the moment I was so pleased with myself that it was all I could do not to start telling my neighbour at the lunch table what I had been up to. It seemed rather unfair, having to keep quiet about my heroics. I felt that I had indeed been both brave and enterprising: I had escaped from Doctor Death and then had returned to outwit him. I had enlisted the Averys as allies, I had sneaked a visit to see Hadley for the purpose of squaring his version of the story with mine, and I had the brainwave of despatching the instructions to the remarkable Mr. Hodman. Can you imagine how hard it was for a boy to resist telling his fellows at least some of this history?

But I had forgotten not only that pride comes before a fall, but more specifically that it was not Galahad who had won the previous game. It was the Friendly Hangman.

When I got back to my desk in the sixth form, the letter was not there. I took out every single book, every single piece of paper, but it wasn't there. *The Arthurian Romances* was missing as well.

I looked in the bookshelves. I asked Abbott and a couple of others who were in the room. It was useless. No one had seen the book.

Then Abbott remembered something.

"Oh yes I forgot," he said, "Tyson was in here just before lunch. He seemed to be looking for something."

So Tyson had it. What devil or genius had prompted him to search my desk? What had caused him to open *The Arthurian Romances*? It seemed impossible, but there it was. I'd lost the instructions, and with them the whole battle. Tyson would know that I'd been lying to him, and he would also catch on to the real nature of *Albion's Dream*. What would he do next? Perhaps get the game back from the Doctor, perhaps simply call me in and insist on the whole story. Either way I was damned, and there was nothing I could do about it. All my resolve, all my energy, just drained away from me.

    The surviving members of the school were organised for a long walk that afternoon. I don't remember where we went, but I do remember the outline of a certain branch against the leaden, lowering sky. Leafless and sapless, it had the shape of a merciless claw hanging over my head.

CHAPTER TEN

HOD

THE summons to Tyson did not come. I scarcely saw the Doctor and Avery's coup, if he was planning one, did not materialise. I felt that I was living under a volcano which, after a period of ominous rumbling, had fallen strangely silent.

Hadley was in the sick room for several more days. I felt too listless to visit him again, and did not even seek news of him. The epidemic began to subside and the routines of school to re-establish themselves. Tyson was more conceited than ever. Only a very sound school, he said, had the morale to endure such difficult circumstances without, as he put it, 'running to Mummy's skirts'. As if to confirm his point, when rugby football was resumed, we beat our old rivals, Ripley Farm, by five tries to one.

Avery was rather subdued, I thought, and it could not have been entirely my imagination that he was avoiding me. He talked to me abruptly and only when he had to, and he even banished me to left wing on the rugby team, a position which he knew I hated.

I was not really surprised. I had not been to see him again since my nocturnal visit, although had no doubt expected me to do so, and he may have thought that my turning up that night, and the story I had brought with me, were based on a fiction that I had later come to regret, and on which he had been led to build unrealistic hopes.

What did puzzle me was Tyson's behaviour. I couldn't understand why he didn't call me in. The very first day after the disappearance of my letter, he came into prayers with his usual sheaf of books and papers under his arm and placed them carefully on his desk. It was the height of the epidemic and I had been 'promoted' to the choir benches. The music master, a bony and sadistic person eager to curry favour with the head, had made it his contribution to the fight against disease to keep up the numbers of the choir. He had even increased the frequency of singing practices. Willy-nilly, certain of us who had always studiously avoided the choir benches – and in my case with good reason – were recruited as choristers, and a very poor sound we produced, I'm sure. But it meant that I had a close view of Tyson's desk, and among his papers was the copy of *The Arthurian Romances*. The pages fitted together tightly, so the offending letter, it seemed, had been removed.

I thought that he had brought the book in for my benefit alone, to let me know that he knew, but it turned out he had another purpose, because after prayers he picked it up and turned to the following passage: "A grave pestilence swept the land, and at Arthur's court alone were measures taken to combat and assuage the evil. The King would hear no talk of the illness, and he expected the same discipline of his knights. Other Kingdoms of the land lost great numbers of their warriors, but to Arthur this merely created the opportunity for more ambitious conquests, and he duly extended his domain at the expense of weaker and less decisive leaders."

I might have blushed for the extraordinary arrogance of the man, for his impertinent comparisons, but at the time I was struck only by how his remarks related to the game. We had been accustomed to identifying Tyson with the Hangman, but clearly he thought of himself as a King, and I remembered that the Hangman in the last game had been victorious only with the King turned up in front of him.

On another occasion I might have been more interested in developing this idea, but I was genuinely tired of the whole business, and I put it from my mind.

Still Tyson didn't summon me. He was waiting for something, but for what?

At last Hadley emerged from the Sick Bay. He looked small and wan. His trousers, which never really fitted him at the best of times, looked far too big for him. He was eager to tell me about Dr. Fell and how he had parried his questions, but I sensed that there was nothing new in the story and cut him short.

Hadley was hurt. "It wasn't my fault that I got ill," he said.

"No, and it wasn't your fault that you blabbed about the game," I replied.

"What do you mean? I didn't blab."

"Huh. You nearly blabbed the lot. Didn't I tell you?"

I hadn't told him, but I did so now—about his coma and his ramblings. I suppose he must have thought that Tyson had come across the game by chance.

"Crikey, I'm sorry," he said.

"Yeah. Well. Can't be helped," I said.

I didn't even mention about my letter to Mr. Hodman. I felt ashamed of the mess I'd made, but I also felt it was my problem alone. I didn't want Hadley's advice.

Half term arrived. There were five days of glorious freedom ahead.

I decided that I would take the game with me, more for reasons of security than because I had any desire to play it.

I took the train from Woking to Gillingham, Dorset. I always loved that ride. I loved train rides anyway, still do, but that particular journey has remained the best of all to me. Sandstone and conifers slowly give way to chalk and the great broadleaves. The towns at first seem drab and dirty, but as you get to the plain even the towns become interesting, quite separate from the countryside, and distinct in their personalities. Basingstoke is better than Woking, Andover than Basingstoke, and Salisbury—well, Salisbury is a real city in its own right, not only because of its great spire, but because of the way it is mistress of its surroundings, like all medieval cities must have been.

And after Salisbury the line reaches the edge of the plain and the West Country begins. Large billboards by the railway proclaim 'You are now entering the STRONG COUNTRY'. When I was younger I thought that Strong referred not to a brand of cider, but to some entirely justifiable provincial pride. The land of Arthur, of Alfred; the West Country that had stood against the Saxons, Wessex that had driven back the Danes.

Can anyone but a boy released from boarding school, or a prisoner on parole, know how long five days can be?

The river was fringed with brittle plates of ice, and even the tufts of grass wore their little icy coronets.

Brandy was ecstatic to see me.

"I'm afraid he hasn't had many really long walks," my mother told me. "It's been so cold that he's had to make do with a quick run around the field."

So we had to make up for that. We went walking morning and afternoon. The shooting season was over, but that didn't matter. I took the same delight in the sudden darting of snipe and flurry of teal, the same pleasure in the call of the pheasant and in the mallard as they beat their way slowly airborne off the river. Perhaps I was secretly glad that I had no gun, for not much later I discovered that there are other ways of alerting yourself to your surroundings than by traipsing about with a weapon, and that nature looks on you with a kindlier eye when you're not engaged in blasting off at bits of her.

Brandy was pleased; he never liked the shooting season.

One morning – it must have been the third day of my reprieve – Brandy and I left home very early. I had my rod, and thought to go after a perch, but the river was low and icy cold and I gave up after a few casts. The day was bright and we decided to venture beyond our usual boundaries. By nine o'clock we were close to Okeford.

I sat down by the hedge to rest and meditated idly. How beautiful the land was in its frosty costume, how perfect everything seemed, how still and perfectly quiet.

I found myself thinking of Mr. Hodman: he would enjoy a day like this. Probably he was tramping through the fields somewhere or other and perhaps not so far away.

I wanted to see him, to talk to him. After all, we were within a few miles of his village.

I began scrutinising the hedge behind me. A hazel shoot caught my eye, slender and perfectly straight. I took out my penknife, laboriously cut it down, and began stripping the bark, which came easily off the wood. In a short while I held a fresh, bright walking stick in my hand: my gift for Mr. Hod. It even had a knob where it needed one.

It was a two hour walk to his village, but it seemed to pass in a moment. Perhaps it was the stick, perhaps it was the morning sunshine after what had seemed like weeks of that grey hood of a sky – at any rate, we climbed Bulbarrow effortlessly and arrived at Mr Hodman's village in the highest of spirits. It was the furthest I had ever been with Brandy, and he seemed to sense this distinction, because he stopped running all over the place in his usual aimless fashion and walked obediently at my heel – something that he never did when I wanted him to.

When we arrived at the village I felt tired. Outside the church was a large, solid bench which looked like a good place for a rest. Brandy was tired too, and lay down under the bench, closed his eyes and went to sleep. I looked round at the church and, although years of compulsory worship had jaded my appetite for all that, I felt the urge to go in. I was attracted, in spite of myself, by the age and grace of the building. The grass surrounding it was brilliant green in the sunshine, the great yews moved ponderously in the breeze. The grey and white stones of the church itself exhibited that particular cleansed brightness that other buildings never seem to have.

I went in. It was very dim, lit only by shafts of sunlight through the stained glass. There was that familiar musty, dusty smell which is the product of stone and dark and age, but with some peculiar sweetness to it as well.

A single worshipper sat in rather a casual fashion against the wall. It was Mr. Hodman.

"What a pleasant surprise," he said. "Were you looking for me?"

I was startled by the coincidence of our meeting. "No. Well, yes. I was going to look for you, but I just happened to come into the church."

"It's a good habit," he said, "to happen to come into churches. They are favourable places for people happening to visit them. Come and sit down for a moment if you like."

I sat near him on the pew. The door creaked open and Brandy appeared, wondering where I had got to. When he saw me he wagged his tail and ambled over.

HOD

"I'm sorry, Mr. Hodman," I got up to take the dog outside.

"It may worry some people to see dogs in churches," he said, "but it doesn't worry me." And he motioned me to sit down again.

"The church near our school has a notice up saying 'No Dogs'– not even in the churchyard I mean."

"I don't think St. Francis would have approved of that, do you?"

I laughed. "No, I don't suppose he would."

"So I daresay we can let your dog stay awhile."

Then he fell silent, and I with him.

As before his silence lasted a long time. Everything about him was on a large scale: his great height, his long silences, the deep emphatic tones of his voice.

He made the sign of the cross and got up to leave. The sunshine outside seemed even more brilliant. I remembered my gift and fetched it from where it lay on the bench.

"This is for you," I told Mr. Hodman.

He was surprised and thoroughly pleased.

"How very kind of you," he said. "But how did you know that I have a passion for walking sticks? You see, it fits me perfectly. I have quite a large collection at home, and each one has a name."

"Your walking sticks have *names*?"

"Yes. I shall have to think of a good name for this one." He thought for a moment. "What about Old Hod?"

I looked at him quickly. He smiled.

"I know that you didn't actually say in your letter that you had cast me in the role of Hod…"

"My letter? You mean you got my letter?"

"Oh yes. It arrived, let me see, about ten days ago, I should say. I read the documents, as you said that I might, and I've given some little thought to the matter. Let's go to my home, shall we, and we'll see about some lunch and I can return the papers to you."

So Tyson had posted my letter. What a fantastic stroke of luck. It had been the book he had been looking for. He had found the letter inside and posted it for me. And then neglected to tell me.

"Had the letter been, er, tampered with at all?"

"No, no, I don't think so. I didn't notice anything odd about it. No torn corners. Do you suspect that somebody got hold of it before it was posted?"

I began telling him the story, but he cut me short.

"I think, Edward, that we'll have something to eat first and the story afterwards. I've always found that a good order for things."

His house was one of those old Dorset labourers' cottages, tiny, low-beamed, whitewashed and thatched. Too small, I felt, for Mr. Hodman, who had to walk around with his head lowered to avoid the beams. For the doorways he almost had to double up.

But it was a fine old place nonetheless, very sparsely furnished for one single, uncommon old man. A chaise-longue was the only 'luxury' in the place. There were a lot of books, and some pictures on the wall, rather surprisingly modern, with bright splashes of colour and strange shapes.

The kitchen was really tiny. We sat at a scrubbed pine table which took up most of the room, and Mr. Hodman served lunch, consisting of huge uneven slices of bread, slabs of cheddar cheese, a pot of homemade pickle and a tin of baked beans. This last was for me, he said. He didn't eat baked beans. He opened the tin, put a spoon in it and placed it on the table.

"I don't suppose you want them heated, do you?"

"No, it's all right," I said, not wishing to put him to any trouble. I'd never eaten cold beans before, but they weren't bad, better than pickle anyway. Mr. Hodman opened himself a bottle of beer and poured me a glass, too. We sat and ate, mostly in silence. Again I was surprised at the old man's appetite. He ate wolfishly, and used the back of his hand to wipe his mouth, cleaning his hand afterwards on the napkin by his side.

When the bread and cheese were finished, he produced two generous slices of apple pie, the best sort of apple pie, the outside of the pastry crisp and brown, the inside soft and sticky, the whole thing covered in large amounts of brown sugar. We helped ourselves from a tin of Cornish clotted cream.

After lunch we did the washing up: a breadknife, two spoons, two glasses and two bowls. The table was wiped and Mr. Hodman left the room, reappearing with the papers from the game in his hand. He put them on the table in front of me, sat down and began lighting his pipe.

The sun had moved to the window directly behind him and he was larger than life in that tiny kitchen with the sun streaming in behind him.

When he was ready he asked to hear "as much of the story as

you want to tell me." So what I did was to fill in the gaps in the narrative of my letter, in particular I giving him a lively account of my dealings with the doctor and the Hangman.

He seemed especially interested in the doctor's words to me that evening in the annexe, and he pressed me to try and remember more carefully what he had said about the origin of the game. I told him what I could.

He then asked me a few questions about Tyson, what he was like with the boys and the staff, how his lessons were, and so on. I suppose I may have exaggerated a little in the portrait I painted, but Tyson, after all, was somebody of exaggerated dimensions and, in spite of all my deference to his authority, I knew that Hadley was right: Tyson was a dangerous man.

It was mid-afternoon and I had a long way to go before dark. Mr. Hodman offered to accompany me part of the way. He selected 'Old Hod' from his stand of walking sticks and off we set. Brandy was waiting where I'd left him, on the front step.

I thought that Mr. Hodman would just a few steps with us, but in the event he climbed right to the top of Bulbarrow, which is a long, steep stretch, without showing the least signs of exertion.

When we parted, he said, "Now I'm not going to give you any more advice, Edward, because I've already given it, and you ignored it, as young men of your age are inclined to do with the words of an old buffer like me. Perhaps quite rightly," he added. "But I will say: be very careful, especially in your dealings with the Doctor. I do not think you are quite out of the woods yet."

With that he said goodbye, and when I turned round, after walking a little further, he was still standing on the same spot on the crown of the hill, with both hands raised in a strange hieratic gesture. It looked like some form of benediction, and that picture of him returned to my mind many times afterwards, always bringing with it a feeling of strength.

I made my way home, joyfully. Now on my own again, I had time to reflect on my extraordinary good luck that Tyson had, after all, posted my letter, and that the secrets of the game were safely in my possession once more. I decided that during the two days of half-term that were left I would sit down and write, in as much detail as I could remember, the history of the games I had played and their consequences.

When I arrived home, I had another surprise awaiting me. My father had come back from his trip during the afternoon and had opened his mail. In it was the letter from me that Dr. Fell had posted and that I had quite forgotten to retrieve.

He asked me to step inside the study with him, and he did not look pleased.

I wasn't exactly frightened of my father—except on the rare occasion when he flew into a rage at some misdemeanour or other—but in some respects I didn't know him very well. He was away in London all week and frequently abroad on business trips. Even at weekends he kept himself busy with his gardening or his papers. We scarcely ever had a serious talk about anything, and when we did it was more like a lecture—too one sided to deserve the label of 'conversation'.

My letter was lying open on his desk. He gestured towards it.

"This letter of yours," he said, "contains some rather disagreeable news. I had thought that the game referred to was lost, long ago."

"Well, it had been lost, Dad, but I found it behind a bookcase in one of the rooms at Turnworth."

"So that's where it got to. Does Jack know you found it?"

"No, I didn't tell him."

"Good. Well then, I think the best thing you could do now is to bring the game here and return it to me. Since the rules have disappeared you could never have learned to play it. It wasn't much of a game in any case."

"What are you going to do with it?" I asked.

"I'll put it there," he said, pointing to the open fire. "Where it belongs."

"The trouble is, Dad," I said, "that I've got it at school. Couldn't it wait for the holidays?"

"All right, but in the meantime just put it out of your mind."

Although I knew exactly why my father had spoken as he had, I wasn't supposed to know, and this gave me the opportunity to probe a bit.

"I don't see why you want to burn it, Dad. It's beautifully drawn, all by hand. It must be quite unique."

"Yes, yes, I know," he said impatiently. "But it needn't concern you why it must be burnt."

Must be burnt. Strong words.

"I can't think what harm it would do to keep it."

"I told you it need not concern you," he said. But it must have occurred to him that he was in danger of simply provoking my further curiosity. "All I'll say is that the game has a history, and not a very happy one," he continued, in a more placatory tone.

"Something to do with Jack, I suppose," I said, and then seeing him start at this I went on quickly. "Since you didn't want me to have mentioned it to him."

"Yes," he said shortly.

"But how could a mere game be so important?" I said. I knew I was pushing my luck a bit, but there was just a chance that I might persuade him to let out a few confidences. And it was a rare moment, having my father's full attention on a subject that interested me so deeply.

He deliberated a few seconds.

"Look, son, more or less your age, that game did have a sort of excitement for me. Some people seemed to think that it was more important than any old board game, but I just enjoyed playing it as you enjoy, say, Monopoly."

"I don't like Monopoly."

"No, well, some other game then."

"Go on."

"I mean, if we had the rules, I'd play it with you now, just to prove there's nothing to it. If we had the game, of course. As one old tramp said to the other: If we had some ham, we could have some ham and eggs, if we had some eggs." He laughed at his own joke.

There was no way I could turn down the chance. Fathers can get angry, they can even be violent, but in the end they are still fathers, and that's a long way from headmasters and doctors with hypodermic syringes.

"And if I told you we've got both ham and eggs?"

He didn't get my meaning for a moment, and when he did I could see the struggle between anger at my deception and the obligation to keep his own word, being fought out in his eyes.

"You've got the game, then?"

"Yes."

"And you've got the rules?"

"Yes."

"Then why the devil did you lie to me, to your own father? I can put up with a lot of things from my children. I can put up with stupidity, with clumsiness, with incompetence and sheer bad manners. But I will not put up with lies."

I had expected something like this: it was the price I had to pay. But it was cheap enough.

"I'd be perfectly within my rights," he went on, "to refuse to play with you. Perfectly justified."

But I didn't think he would refuse.

"And what's this letter all about?" he said. "If you have the instructions, why were you writing to ask me for them?"

"There seem to be some pages missing," I said.

"Bring them here. And the game," he said.

I went up to my bedroom to get the game. While I was there I took the papers from my pocket and detached all but the last page of my father's letter, which is where the instructions started. I also removed Hadley's Hangman card from the set.

My father was unmistakably curious to see the game again. It must have been years since he had last set eyes on it. Clearly the memories it brought back were not all bad, for he took it from me eagerly enough. He looked first at the instructions and, noting that only the very end of his letter had survived, he seemed relieved.

"There is something missing, isn't there, Dad? There was a letter you had written."

He was looking at the pages I'd given him.

"There was a letter, yes. Your mother must have destroyed it. She seems to have been the last to handle the game."

"Why should she have done that?"

"I don't know." You see, adults also tell lies when it suits them. "Look, if you insist on playing, we'll have one game. But after that the whole caboodle goes on the fire, agreed?"

"Don't you think it really belongs to me now?" I asked cautiously. "Finders keepers, you know. And isn't that what Mum's note says, – 'for someone else to find.' Well, It was me who found it."

"Have you been playing the game at school?" he asked.

"Yes."

"Then you must have ignored one of the first instructions. The game is not supposed to be played outside the family."

"I've been playing it with John Hadley."

"So?"

"He's my cousin."

"Oh yes, I suppose he is. Tell me truthfully now, have you or John noticed anything odd about the game?"

"No. What do you mean?"

He didn't bother to answer my question. "I always thought it was Jack's imagination. You'd better keep the game, I suppose, but if ever—if ever—playing it produces any disturbing results, you must put it away at once and come and tell me about it. I know it's a bit difficult for you to understand why I should make this condition, so you'll have to take it on trust. Maybe when you're older I'll be able to explain more clearly."

"I hope so," I said. I avoided promising to abide by this condition, but my father took it that I had.

"Now," he said. "Let's play. You set the game out. I'll be back in a minute."

I felt excited at the prospect of playing with him, though I wished we could have played with all our cards, so to speak, on the table.

He came back. "I told your mother that you and I needed some time to talk a few things over. So we won't be disturbed. Oh, yes, that's another condition. Don't talk to your mother about the game. Or to Jack."

We started playing. My father always enjoyed games, they stimulated his competitive instinct. It was a very different matter from playing with Hadley. My father went at things boldly and confidently. He drew the Merchant and occupied the Coast. From there he began attacking the other citadels of the First Kingdom and amassing tokens. He drew the Hangman and the King was turned up to him. Following a plan of my own, I ignored the First Kingdom, drew Galahad and occupied the Dungeon. My father's tactic was immediately to attack me on the Dungeon with all the powers he had amassed in the First Kingdom. A war of attrition was fought and I lost possession of my fortress, barely escaping with the help of Hermes.

But he soon attacked me again. He showed no interest in progressing towards the centre of the board. His idea of the game was to concentrate his powers and use them to vanquish his opponent.

Again Galahad only just escaped, this time losing Hermes. With neither mage nor guide, he had little chance of entering the Third Kingdom. My father had exchanged his First Kingdom pieces and some of his tokens for a warrior and a guide, and with these he hunted me down and captured me.

We probably played for no more than an hour. My father had enjoyed himself and was pleased, as always, at winning. He was in an excellent humour.

"There you are, you see. Just a game, and not a bad one either. Better than Monopoly, you're right about that. Your mistake, you know, was not to gather strength in the First Kingdom. In fact you played rather like Jack used to, and I generally beat him as well. He also had the idea that getting near the centre was what the game was about, but no one ever gets to the centre: the game isn't won that way. Power and position in the First Kingdom, that's the secret. Anyway, the game's yours. Make what you will of it."

I too had enjoyed the game. My father's robust and uncomplicated urge to win was rather a relief, in fact, and I was not surprised to find that the moves we had made found no reflection in the events of my life. I wondered whether it was the state of mind of the player, rather than any actual force deriving from the game, that was decisive.

CHAPTER ELEVEN

THE CAMP AND THE DOLE

BEFORE I returned to school I wrote the promised account of all my dealings with the game. I made a copy of the instructions to have with me at school, and the original instructions, my father's letter and my own account I hid in the nook behind my picture of the Chinaman.

I wished that I didn't have to go back to school for the rest of term, but I knew that the battle against the Doctor and the Hangman was unresolved and had to be played out. I felt in a strong position, with the game properly my own for the first time and with Hod's blessing vivid in my mind.

When I saw Hadley I told him of all the events he had missed during his illness and after. He had been hurt by my abruptness to him a week before, but now he understood how it had been caused by my worry over the fate of my letter to Mr. Hodman.

He, too, was eager to play again. We both wished to try and rid ourselves of Dr. Fell and to continue our plan of scotching Tyson. He was particularly excited at what I now told him of Avery's response to my story about the Doctor.

"What if we could get rid of Tyson, and make Avery headmaster instead?" he said.

We decided that for the next game, which I had made up my mind would be the last one I would play with Hadley, we must identify all the characters in the pack with a living person and that Hadley must extend and improve his map of the school so that we would know exactly what we were doing when we played. We talked a lot about how we could guarantee our victory which, for the first time, we began to think of clearly as the victory of good over evil. The most important thing was to know who was on our side. Hod, Merlin, Galahad, Pellinore, Puck and Christ – the last of whom we decided to leave without a corresponding character (although in my mind he was always linked with my brother Ben and my Uncle Jack) – these were allies. Death and the Hangman, obviously, were against us. Hadley offered to make a new Queen card, so that we could also have the support of Miss Daphne.

"Yes, but don't make it look like her. It must be a picture of the Good Woman, or something like that."

"The White Goddess."

"If you like. And for heaven's sake don't give her a beard."

That still left a number of significant characters unaccounted for: the Judge, the Priest, the Soldier, Zoroaster, Thor, and Hermes. We examined these cards in turn and racked our brains for suitable candidates. The Judge, Hadley thought, bore a remote resemblance to the Chairman of the Board of Governors of the school, whom

THE CAMP AND THE DOLE

I had never seen and he had only seen once: but the figure of the Judge seemed anyway suitable to his position.

After this we got stuck. The remaining cards had never played a significant part in our game, perhaps because we tended to discard them and play the cards we knew, and perhaps because of the uncanny properties of the game itself. So in the end we realised that our only option was, as far as possible, to continue as before and avoid those characters who were still unknown quantities.

We were now ready to play. The Queen card was finished and took her place in the pack and Hadley had extended his map. I thought that he had slightly bent the lines to suit his idea, but at least it gave us something to work on. The Rings, as Tyson's study, and the Dole, as Death's lair, were to be avoided. The Camp and the Hermitage should be favourable. The Dungeon, at a stretch, could be seen as the sixth form and the Healing Stone as our dormitory.

"The healing powers of sleep," said Hadley.

I suggested that we fix a date for Tuesday – my best day, and also one with no lessons in the afternoon. We would play in the safety of the woods, weather permitting.

In the course of Tuesday morning I received a message to go to Miss Daphne's dispensary. She was not there, but the Doctor was. He looked rather ill, and in spite of a superficial cheerfulness, I could see he was in a mean mood.

"I'm surprised you haven't been to see me, young Yeoman."

"I've been rather busy, sir, and I wasn't sure where to find you."

The epidemic was a thing of the past and, with only the usual coughs and sniffles to treat, the Doctor was no longer a daily visitor to the school.

"Yes. But you have good news for me, I hope?"

"I'm afraid not, sir."

"What do you mean?"

"I saw my father at half-term, of course, and he said he had no idea where the rules of play had got to. In fact, he didn't seem to want to talk about the game at all."

"He didn't eh? I suppose he wouldn't," he added quietly. "Well, in that case we must think of another plan."

My heart sank. I don't know why I had imagined that he would let me off so easily.

"Perhaps the best thing would be for me to invite you to tea at my house one day later this week."

"Oh, I don't think I'd be able to get permission to do that, sir," I said quickly.

"There won't be any problems on that score," he said. "Mr. Tyson feels most indebted to me at present and, after all, I am an old friend of the family." He paused. "So you will come to tea on, let's say, Friday. And we will play the game together."

"But…without the instructions?"

"Never mind them. We will do what we can. I have learnt something of what the game is about, and I am sure you have learnt other things. No doubt together we will learn a little more."

The thought of being alone with Dr. Fell in his own house disturbed me profoundly.

He must have seen this and been frightened of losing his prey, so he relaxed in his chair and placed the fingertips of one hand against those of the other, spreading them out like a fan. It is a gesture I have seen elsewhere, and I suppose it is meant to be a sign of concentration, but it always struck me as utterly vacuous.

"I think," said Dr. Fell, "that to be fair to you, I ought to let you know some of my conclusions about this game. What we are dealing with here, you and I, is a piece of highly sophisticated magic." He dropped his voice theatrically on the last word. He may even have believed that this word alone would be enough to lure me to any sort of adventure, so little did he understand. "Yes, magic. The game is capable of—how shall I put it—exerting an influence on the world around us. In the wrong hands it would be capable of evil. In the hands of a savant, however, such as myself, it is equally capable of good. To such ends, when I have properly mastered the formulae, I propose to apply it."

He had a look of extraordinary smugness on his face.

"You may wonder how it is that I, a Doctor, should concern myself with the so-called occult. I will tell you. While a student at university, I became interested in such matters. I read widely and grew familiar with certain of the archetypal symbols and their values. I underwent harsh disciplines in order to cleanse and prepare myself for the strenuous calling of magician. Looking back at that time in my life, however, I can only suspect that someone or something was working against my success. At any rate, I found myself unable to bring my studies to any sort of conclusion. I chose to become a doctor, knowing that in ancient times the Doctor of the spirit and the Doctor of the body were one and the same. Although I say it myself, I became a very able doctor, and at times my knowledge of metaphysical forces was a decided asset. I did not ever relinquish my ambition to learn the hidden ways of power, but inevitably, as the years passed, it became more of a hobby, less of a burning ambition. I have in my acquaintance a number of practitioners of the occult arts, and among them is a lady adept at divining fortunes. One evening at her house she told me that I was destined to make a discovery, one that would be capable of changing my life. She could not, she said, be sure of the precise nature of this discovery, but it was to come to me through the agency of a child, and it would take the form of an ancient legacy of our land."

I sat absolutely rigid, absolutely silent. I didn't want, by the least movement, to interrupt the flow of his words. And I was still deeply afraid of him, and of what he might do to me if he came to believe that I was thwarting his purposes.

"I took the vacant position at this school, not of course because I have any particular fondness for the mewlings and pukings of young boys—quite the reverse—but because I felt I should put myself in contact with children, and some intuition told me that here is where my destiny lay. The rest you know.

"I would like you to consider yourself a privileged partner in my designs. I do not ultimately need you, you understand, but you can

THE CAMP AND THE DOLE

be of some small service to me and I will reward you accordingly. For a start, the game has to be played by two people, and I am loth to involve any of my own acquaintance in this enterprise. You cannot imagine," he finished, "the extent of the riches and power which will come to us if only we can fathom the true potential of the game."

He sat back, waiting for my answer. I wanted to say something helpful, conciliatory – but what?

"Listen to me carefully, Yeoman. With you or without you, I will pursue my plans. If you refuse to help me, then I shall be obliged to… puncture your credibility. This I can do quite simply. I will give Tyson a carefully edited version of what has been going on. There is no doubt that he will believe me. I will indicate to him that you and your friend Hadley have been involved in an attempt to employ the forces of darkness – I do not think that will be too fanciful a description for his simple mind – to destroy him as headmaster of this school."

I must have started at this for he laughed that chilling laugh of his and said, "Oh yes, friend Hadley let out a number of things that I omitted to mention to you, including allusions to your plot against the headmaster. You do not seriously believe, do you, that I would wish to enlist your help if I did not know that you had yourself begun to exploit the deeper possibilities of the game? I will convince Tyson of this, and he will expel you from the school."

In spite of this threat, I experienced a surge of relief. If he thought that expulsion held even the slightest terror for me, compared to what I felt at the prospect of falling under his evil sway, then he had another think coming.

I got up.

"Do your worst," I said. And, for the second time, I fled his presence.

That afternoon Hadley and I played the game. I had not told Hadley of my meeting with the Doctor, although I'm not sure why. I don't think it was to save him anxiety. Perhaps it was that I preferred not to think about it myself. If I was on the edge of an abyss, I reacted by closing my eyes.

The weather was fine: the wind had moved to the west and it was warmer. Tom's camp had a deserted, rather forlorn air, and I insisted that we spend some time clearing sodden leaves and improving the earthworks. Then we spread our raincoats on the ground and set out the game.

Hadley drew the Hangman, so we agreed that he should play for the 'villains'. For a while we dallied uneventfully in the First Kingdom. I concentrated on collecting the characters I wanted. I got Galahad and Merlin, and then I had the chance to draw for a guide. I hoped for Hod but drew Puck.

"Damn," I said.

"Best card in the pack," said a voice, not Hadley's.

I started to my feet and was astonished to see none other than Charlie Tom, laughing merrily at me from the depths of a rhododendron bush.

"I thought this was where you must be," said Tom, extricating himself from the foliage.

I didn't know whether to be pleased to see him, or angry at the rude shock he had given me. Neither did Hadley.

"Why can't you just arrive like any normal person?" said Hadley. "Why do you insist on creeping up and scaring us out of our wits?"

"Just testing you," said Tom. "I was wondering whether either of you are learning anything useful from these games of yours. Like how to keep your eyes open. As I thought, you aren't."

He looked tremendous, very fit and a bit bigger somehow, although that may have been the result of his being out of school uniform, for he had on a pair of jeans and a jersey instead of the ridiculous short-trousered grey flannel suits that we were condemned to wear.

"It's good to see you, Tom," I said. "But what the hell are you doing here anyway? I shouldn't let Tyson catch you."

"I just came to see you two and a couple of other people, and to stir up a bit of trouble if possible." He took out his Gold Leaf cigarettes. I accepted one, but Hadley didn't.

"Vile things," he said, blowing his nose.

"What sort of trouble did you have in mind, Tom?" I asked him.

"Oh, nothing in particular. Thought I'd distribute a few smokes, and, oh yes, I let the air out of the tyres of Tyson's car as I came in. And another one next to it, a little red job."

"The doctor's," I murmured.

"Oh, the doctor's is it? Well, teachers, doctors – all the same, aren't they, really? Don't mind me, go on with your game. I'll just have a scout round the old woods. See you in a minute."

And off he went, swift and quiet, utterly at home.

"Why did he say, 'best card in the pack,' Yeoman? Did you tell him he was Puck?"

I was sure I hadn't done any such thing. "I suppose he just liked the card – instinctively, I mean."

"OK. But look what happened. You drew the Puck card, and he arrived that same instant. Do you think the effect of the game might be speeding up?"

It was rather an alarming thought.

"Don't be silly," I said. "Let's play."

So we did.

Puck, Merlin and Galahad occupied the Camp. Hadley kept the Hangman on the Rings, but he was throwing high and began to collect tokens. The King was turned up to him and soon he drew a warrior, Thor, who immediately led the Hangman and the King out of the Rings in search of new conquests.

"Don't attack me here," I said. "Go for another fortress."

"I'll do my best," said Hadley.

But we couldn't go against the dice and it brought the Hangman and Thor inexorably to the Camp. I threw disastrously. Puck was defeated by Thor and Merlin was captured by the Hangman. Galahad barely escaped.

Tom reappeared. "Someone's been cutting trees," he said. "Perfectly good ones, too. How's the game going?"

THE CAMP AND THE DOLE

"Why aren't you at school, Tom?" I asked him. "Don't you go to school?"

"Not at the moment," he said, but there was something evasive in his tone.

"What do you mean 'not at the moment,'" Hadley pressed him. "Either you do or you don't."

Tom was embarrassed. "I do go, but I don't at the moment. What does it matter to you anyway," he finished, irritably.

This line of questioning made Tom uncomfortable, and it must have made him careless too, for otherwise I'm sure he wouldn't have been caught off-guard by what followed.

None of us heard them coming. They must have crept up remarkably quietly for two such large men. The first we knew of their arrival was the sound of one of Tyson's angriest bellows.

"There he is," he yelled. "Get him, Garth."

For Mr. Garth was there too, all six foot of him.

Tom was off, scampering through the bushes. Hadley and I sat frozen to the spot.

"And the game, again, I see," said Tyson meatily. Without another word, and pushing me peremptorily out of the way, he bent down and gathered the pieces. He folded the board, crammed everything into the box and put it under his arm. I had been about to throw. The dice were still in my hand and I slipped them into my pocket.

Garth was returning, with Tom held by the scruff of the neck.

"Got the blighter," he said with satisfaction.

I'd thought that Tom would get away, with his impish speed and his knowledge of the woods, but I'd forgotten the moves that had just been played. Tom didn't stand a chance.

Mr. Garth was the temporary science master. He'd arrived at the beginning of term to fill a gap. He was the biggest man I'd ever set eyes on – not only immensely tall but broad with it. Thor.

Tyson dismissed Hadley and me to our dormitory.

"I'll be dealing with you later," he said, leaving us in no doubt as to the nature of that interview. But Tom was his first concern.

I have to hand it to Tom. He was brave. As he was dragged off, he called back to us. "I would have made it," he said, "but I tripped."

Garth cuffed him over the head, but Tom hadn't finished. "Don't worry about me," he said, "there's nothing they can do to me." And Garth cuffed him again, harder. And we could see that this one really hurt.

"We've got one chance," I told Hadley, "the Doctor."

"The *Doctor*? Don't be stupid. We're for it."

"I'll see you in the dormitory," I said. "If Tyson comes for us before I get back, tell him I had an upset stomach and went to the loo."

I had no time to explain.

The red car was in the car park, standing on flat tyres. The Doctor was still in the school.

I ran to the dispensary. The door was open, and there he was, packing his bag. He looked at me sharply.

"Thank goodness I'm not too late," I said.

"For what?" he said coolly.

"To tell you I've changed my mind."

"You are too late," he said. "I've decided that I can do quite well without you."

"I don't think you can," I said, my heart in my mouth. "You see, I lied to you. I know the rules of the game."

I had him, I could tell instantly.

"I see," he said. "This does put a different complexion on things. Am I to understand that the rules are in your possession?"

"Not actually in writing," I said, "but I got them from my father at half-term, as much as he could remember."

"You little liar," he said, but it was said without rancour. "I suppose you hoped to keep them to yourself. But why the sudden change of mind?"

I decided that I had to tell him at least part of the truth.

"Tyson's got my game. He's confiscated it. He'll probably burn it. He found us playing. I don't know what he'll do now. We'll be lucky if we get off with a beating."

"So you did bring back the original version – and now you've lost it, which means I've got the only copy. Well, well."

He seemed to deliberate. I thought he might still decide he was better off without me, and so I went on.

"Yes, but the point is your copy is incomplete."

"What do you mean?" he said fiercely.

"There's a card missing."

"And you've got it, I suppose."

"Yes."

"But not with you, of course."

"No."

"But you'll bring it on Friday, I trust."

"I'm afraid we'll have to play sooner than that, sir. As things have turned out."

"Yes, yes. Maybe you're right."

"Perhaps now I really had better be ill for a while."

"Yes. Right again. You're an excellent little schemer, Yeoman, I must say."

I told him of the message I had left with Hadley.

"An upset stomach, eh? Fine. We don't need a needle for that, do we? A couple of these pills should have you running nicely. Not enough to make you uncomfortable, I hope."

His little laugh.

I took the pills he offered, and popped them in my mouth.

"A glass of water, please sir," I said, lisping as the pills slipped around my tongue. He turned to fetch me some water and the pills were out, clenched in my hand. I drank the water.

"Straight to bed, then," he said cheerfully. "I'll go and let Miss Daphne know. And I'll square Tyson for you if I get the chance. Otherwise, *you'll* have to." He laughed again. "By the way, I think the annexe will suit us best, don't you? I'll tell Miss Daphne that there's been a stomach bug around and that I want you in isolation. Now listen." He looked at me penetratingly, holding my eyes deliberately and rigidly with his own. "I'll come this evening, late, and I'll bring the game with me and we'll play. But if there's any thought in your mind of tricking me, then forget it because I'm not a fool and it would profoundly annoy me to be monkeyed with. Do you follow my meaning?"

I did, and I said so.

I was left alone. A little later Miss Daphne came up the stairs and into the dispensary.

"I'm sorry to hear you're not feeling well," she said, looking at me closely.

What a difference between her eyes and those of the doctor. "By George, you *don't* look well," she said. "Come on, off with those clothes."

I was issued with a pair of sickroom pyjamas, an enamel bowl, a towel and a hot water bottle. The bed in the annexe was made and I was given a cup of tea, strong, black and sweet – the only way I like to drink it.

CHAPTER TWELVE

THE BATTLE FOR THE RINGS

MY first visitor was Tyson. He stormed in.

"If you think you can get off the hook by feigning illness," he said, without preamble, "then you're underestimating me, Yeoman, and that's a dangerous mistake."

I didn't sit up. I hoped I looked as ill as he made me feel.

"I really don't feel well, sir. I'm sorry, sir."

"You'd better be. Hadley's already tasted the wrong end of one of my canes and it's my guess he's feeling a lot iller than you at this minute. However, if you insist on continuing this pretence, I can wait. But to the charge of lying to me, to that of disregarding my clear instructions, to that of breaking bounds and to that of consorting with a -" he searched for a word sufficiently weighty to describe the loathsome Tom, "- an outlaw, I will simply add the charge of malingering. So you'd better be really well before you next visit my study, otherwise you may not leave it in an upright position."

With that he left. It wasn't good news, but it was no worse than I'd expected. With my backside safely ensconced in the clean sheets of my sickbed and with a far more serious ordeal in the offing, I was not particularly frightened by his barking. Anyway, I had noticed that something had altered in my relationship with Tyson. It had been happening gradually, but now I knew it for sure. He no longer had the capacity to make me truly afraid. Perhaps it was just the comparison with the dread Dr. Fell, but it seemed to me that there was more to it than that. I no longer believed in Tyson's absolute authority over me. I no longer set store by old fiction of 'in loco parentis'. I had lately spent a great many hours facing up to the most extreme circumstances of my life and it was getting harder to scare me, harder to convince me that rules and hierarchies were what really mattered.

At about nine o'clock that evening the door opened. It was Miss Daphne. She had done her rounds of the junior dormitories and I was her last call. She seemed to be prepared to stay for a while.

"I've brought you a cup of tea," she said. "It's just the thing for stomach troubles. And I've brought a cup for myself, as well. How are you feeling?"

"Not too bad, Miss Daphne."

"Good. Well enough for a game of dominoes?"

"Not really, thank you." The thought of any kind of game made me feel queasy. "But I'd love you to stay for a while."

"Of course, dear. I've even brought my knitting with me. The doctor said he might call in late to have a look at you. Not that I think it's necessary, of course, but he's very conscientious." The way she said 'conscientious' made it seem like a mild insult, as if

THE BATTLE FOR THE RINGS

conscientiousness were a quality that did not necessarily make a person a good doctor. I felt that she didn't much care for Doctor Fell and that pleased me.

We settled down comfortably with a cup of tea. I was very fond of Miss Daphne. She had this extraordinary red hair which she kept tied up in a bun and her face, no longer young, was covered with freckles. Only once in five years had I seen her with her hair down. She used to sleep next door to the dormitory of the youngest boys, of whom I had at one time been the very youngest. Someone was suddenly and violently sick in the night, the door that led to her room opened and she came dashing in with a little torch. Her hair was hanging free, and the auburn locks actually reached her waist.

I felt bold enough to ask her something that I had always wondered about and never dared to mention.

"Miss Daphne?"

"Yes?"

"Miss Daphne, why didn't you ever get married?"

She blushed, but she wasn't really embarrassed. She stopped knitting, though.

"The man I loved died during the war."

"But after that, wasn't anyone else good enough for you?"

"No," she said. 'There was nobody else."

Some minutes later she got up to go.

"I don't expect the doctor will call at this hour," she said. "You'd better settle down and get some sleep. Have a good night's rest and I'm sure you'll feel better in the morning." She smoothed my pillow and tucked in my bedclothes. The words and the action reminded me of my mother. It was one of these simple rituals which, however often repeated, never fail to have their intended, soothing effect.

"Good night," she said.

"Good night, Miss Daphne."

She opened the door to leave and there stood the Doctor.

"Ah, Miss Daphne," he said, evidently a little surprised. "How is our patient?"

"Quite well, I think, Doctor," she replied. "Fancy you calling as late as this."

"Yes, well, I just thought I'd have a quick look at him, you know. There have been these reports, and it's always a good idea to be on the safe side."

"You know best, Doctor, I'm sure," she said. "Good night."

And the Doctor and I were alone.

He seemed distracted and was looking rather dishevelled, but without further ado he opened his bag and took out the game.

"You set it up," he said.

While I did so, he went to the door and listened. Very slowly and carefully, he turned the key in the lock. Then he lit the gas fire, which Miss Daphne had recently extinguished, delved into his bag again and pulled out a small flask, from which he took a swig.

When he came over and sat in the chair by the bed, I noticed he was smelling strongly of whisky. Obviously the flask had been in use earlier that evening.

THE BATTLE FOR THE RINGS

"Now," he said. "How does this damn thing work?"

I explained to him that Hadley and I had been interrupted during a game, and that it was one of the instructions that a game cannot be left unfinished. Did he agree, I asked, to continue Hadley's hand? To my surprise, he raised no objection—in fact I saw that he lacked his usual alertness, which made things easier for me. I reminded him that there was a card missing from the set and explained to him which one it was.

I got him to find a piece of paper and label it 'The Friendly Hangman' as a temporary expedient. While he did this I added my own dice to the set and then laid out the board as it had been that afternoon: the Hangman and Thor with the King at the Camp, and Galahad on his own.

"Aha! The young Galahad," said the Doctor. "But where is my piece?"

"You're playing Thor and the Hangman. And you've got the King as well."

"Yes, but where is my own special piece? Where is Death?"

"In the pack with the rest."

"How can I get hold of him?"

"He gets turned up to you. Otherwise you can find him here or here." I pointed to the Dole and to Devilish. "But you don't want him, you know. He'll kill your other characters."

"That's not important. The point is, can he then continue on his own?"

I wasn't sure of the answer to this. Nobody ever wanted to hold on to Death. He turned up, did his deed, and was returned to the pack. It had never occurred to me that the Doctor would actually welcome his identification with the Death card, but I couldn't have been more wrong.

"Listen," he said. "The Death card in the original pack looks like me, doesn't it?"

"Yes, it does rather."

"And in your game with Hadley I was Doctor Death, right?"

"Yes."

"Well you must have understood enough about the game to know that these resemblances and so-called coincidences are the clues to its power."

"I suppose so."

"So clearly I must play Death."

I said nothing. It was a frightening notion, and I doubted that the rules allowed Death to be played in the same way as other characters, but I did not fancy opposing the doctor's scheme and there was also the possibility that in the end it would work to my advantage.

"I'm not interested in your petty battles, Yeoman. I don't give a hang for your headmaster or for your schoolfellows. The object of the game is to gain the centre, isn't it?"

"That's one way of winning, yes."

"It's not just one way of winning you fool, it's *the* way. All the rest is trivial. You don't understand this game yet. You don't know what *Albion's Dream* is."

"No, I don't."

"Well, I'll tell you. The dream of Albion is *mastery*. Mastery of the forces that control our lives, mastery of the destinies of people. And to gain the centre is to be given a key to this mastery. I will find a way to get to the centre, and then I will embark on the particular manipulations that I have in mind."

He was carried away with his schemes, but he must have realised that he was letting me see his real intentions.

"When I say manipulations, of course I'm referring to the struggle against Evil, the struggle for Good."

I said nothing.

He went on quickly. "Never mind all that now. The point is that Death is the most powerful card in the pack, and I am identified with Death. So I must get hold of the card. And you must help me."

"I think you'll have to wait for it to turn up. Unless you go and seek Death in the Fourth Kingdom. But you'll need a guide to do that."

"Well, we'll see. Come on, let's start."

Thor, the Hangman and the King made for the Rings. I explained to the Doctor that it was the Hangman's favourite place and that there lay his best chance of obtaining the tokens which would allow him through the Toll-Gate into the Second Kingdom.

Galahad was lucky. He was joined by Pellinore and the Queen was turned up to him. I decided that with two warriors I should make an attack on the Rings while I had the advantage, but the

THE BATTLE FOR THE RINGS

Hangman, too, was throwing high and for a while I could make no headway. Then I drew the Merchant and the Judge and defeated Thor. Immediately afterwards I lost the Queen, the King won over the loyalties of the Judge and the Merchant, and I was in trouble.

At this point the Doctor had the opportunity to draw a character card. I held my breath, because a lot depended on which one he got. He was aware of it too, and hesitated.

"Watch *this*," he said in a fierce whisper, and suddenly thrust his head towards me over the table. The effect was, of course, that I didn't actually see him take up the card. It seemed to me that he covered the pack and then raised his hand with an abrupt gesture that brought the card up with its face towards me. It was Death.

He seemed to know this without looking at it himself. Exactly how he produced it, I'm not sure, but I felt that it had been by some sleight of hand. If so it was a masterly conjuring trick.

At all events, there lay the Death card and the Doctor had got what he wanted.

"Now things are on the move," he said. "What do I do now?"

"You throw the red dice. Anything but the skull and Death returns to the pack."

"And we don't want that happening, do we, now?" he said cheerily. He seemed utterly confident as he picked up the red dice and shook it rhythmically in his cupped hands. Did he murmur something to himself as he shook it? I may have imagined it.

The dice hardly rolled at all and stopped with the skull face up. Doom.

"And now the white dice," I said.

A one.

"Let's kill off the King," he said pleasantly.

With the King gone, I soon won back the Judge and the Merchant, and it was only a matter of time before the Hangman was defeated. According to the rules the game was over, but the doctor had not returned Death to the pack and obviously had no intention of doing so. Instead he began moving towards the Toll-Gate. I just let him go. I had no desire to challenge Death and in any case, from this point on, the rules couldn't really cope with the situation. Death was at large on the board and it seemed that nothing could stop him. The doctor seemed to be able to throw whatever he liked with the red dice. He used the mages and warriors to open the passes for him, and then discarded them, continuing with Death alone.

For a while I stayed quietly on the Rings, but when I judged that it was safe I proceeded with Galahad, leaving my other pieces behind. Soon I drew Merlin and, later, Puck. I was throwing well but I kept at a reasonable distance from the doctor, who seemed to pay no attention to the movements of my pieces, impatiently grabbing up the dice as soon as I'd had my throw.

He was drinking, too. At first he'd kept the flask in his bag, but after a while he set it on the table and more and more often took a swig from it. If he'd been sober, perhaps he would have rounded on me and finished me off.

"No one else would have dared to play this piece," he said once.

"Look at him: he's unstoppable. Lucky that you two boys should have cast me in this role. I might never have thought of it."

By the time he entered the Fourth Kingdom I was close behind him. Now, especially, the fact that he was playing Death made it very easy. Neither the Dole nor Devilish held any fears for either of us.

He located the Dragon Time and challenged him. Once again I played the part of the Dragon and once again I lost. Death made three correct guesses and entered the Giant's Grave, the void at the centre.

The doctor sat there staring at the board with glazed eyes. Very quietly I picked up my two dice and slid them under the pillow.

At last he shook himself and sat back. He reached for the flask but it was empty and he dropped it casually into his bag.

"A most satisfactory result, Yeoman." He began collecting the pieces and returning them to the box. "I don't think I shall have any trouble from now on. I've fought the Dragon Time and defeated him." He leant forward and looked at me oddly. "Who knows," he said, "perhaps I've taken the first step towards immortality." And he laughed.

He got up and began packing his bag. "I probably shan't require your help anymore," he said. "But of course I shall be seeing you and there may be a few little points to discuss. Meanwhile, let me bid you goodnight. And please set your mind at rest; the game will not concern you from now on."

He unlocked the door and left, and I breathed a sigh of relief. I tried to unravel the threads of the game we had played. It was true that the Hangman had lost, but Death had won. Or had he? Was the game deprived of its power when the rules were flouted? It had the air of a travesty, Death's mad rush for the centre, but something about the doctor's obsession and his extraordinary control of the dice made me suspect that it was much more than that.

Death had defeated Time. Immortality—wasn't that what the doctor had said?

I grew sleepy, Death and Time chasing each other round in my head. Death defeats Time: everlasting Life…or everlasting Death?

CHAPTER THIRTEEN

THE FALL OF THE KING

MISS Daphne let me sleep the next morning. When I woke it was late. The tiny window of the annexe provided but small clue to the state of the day outside, only that it was grey and dull. But I knew that I had missed most of the morning.

In truth I did not feel well. I felt listless and worn, and reluctant to think about the real world of anger and greed. There were half a dozen books on a shelf within reach of the bed. One of them was the *Nonsense Omnibus* of Edward Lear – the gift, I read, of some grateful parent. And I immersed myself in the unaccountable antics of this parade of melancholy clowns, in the hopeless yearnings of the Yongy Bongy Bo and the Dong with the luminous nose, and in the geography of the Hills of the Chankly Bore.

Tyson did not call on me that day, although Miss Daphne told me that he had asked after my health. She herself took my imagined complaint quite seriously, as if understanding that there was indeed something wrong, even if it had little to do with my stomach.

I slept again in the afternoon and awoke at dusk, which arrived at the little window like a gloved hand. I picked up Edward Lear again, but his characters now seemed more dreadful than comic.

THE FALL OF THE KING

Miss Daphne brought me her radio to listen to and there was a radio play in which ten passengers got stranded for the night at an isolated railway station on the Southern line. During the night one of them dies.

I turned it off, but even the ensuing silence was full of threat. I missed my mother. The hundred miles that separated us might just as well have been a thousand. I imagined what she would be doing now: feeding the dogs and cats, tidying the kitchen, putting logs on the fire, thinking of me, perhaps and of my brother and sisters. And all that remained to me was a sense of her loneliness, and my own.

At about eight-thirty the Doctor arrived. He did not have his bag with him.

"Tyson has called a meeting. You and Hadley are to be expelled."

Mercifully, it seemed a long way off, this sentence. I closed my eyes.

"I thought you would be concerned," said the Doctor.

I said nothing.

"You see it's not just you and the game. He's got wind of something, some plot against him, I don't know precisely what. But you're to be the scapegoats. He told me all this quite openly. I think he needed a friendly ear to confide in. Somebody is out to get him and he's going to bring things to a head in his own way. He's quite determined."

I saw it all clearly. The expulsion of Hadley, a scholar, and of me, a sportsman and a favourite, would be an unprecedented act. In the execution of it Tyson would be taking the sting out of some other threat to his position – a threat that I supposed must come from Avery and the rest of the staff.

"He's aiming to make a public example of you, and when I say public I mean that he's gone to the trouble of arranging a trial for you."

"A trial?" I pictured a courtroom, benches, wigs and a hammer.

"He wants me to be there, and the governors, some senior members of staff and, I believe, your parents."

"When?" I just wished it to be as far away as possible.

"He asked me how soon you would be well enough to attend. It was just a matter of form that he did so, because I don't think he believes there's anything wrong with you. Which there isn't." He paused. "Particularly since you didn't even take the pills I gave you."

"I did."

"You'd have to be a better conjurer than you are to deceive me so easily," he said. "But it was a good try and I can't help admiring it. In fact," he continued, "I've come to think that you're a pretty good performer for your age."

He was looking at me, for the first time, with something like genuine sympathy.

"Perhaps we could still be useful to each other, you and I."

"I don't need you," I said sulkily.

"I could help you," he said. "And you could help me. Anyway," he added, preparing to leave, "I told your headmaster that you needed a couple of days to recover, so he's organised the meeting for Friday evening. I don't expect we'll see each other before then which will give you plenty of time to make up your mind."

I didn't know what he meant by that, but I didn't care either. As soon as he left I went back to Edward Lear. I felt a greater affinity than ever with the Yongy Bongy Bo and I resolved that, as soon as my present ordeal was over, I would set sail for the hills of the Chankly Bore, and that I would go alone.

I slept a lot, those two days, and, as is the way of the bedridden, I grew weak and shaky. Miss Daphne was quite anxious about me. On Friday morning she told me Mr. Tyson wanted to see me that evening. Obviously she had an idea that the situation was serious.

"What have you been up to, Edward?" she asked me. "The Headmaster's always been pleased with you, I thought."

I was less shy with her than I used to be.

"What do you think of Mr. Tyson, Miss Daphne?" I asked.

She stiffened as if ready to censure this breach of etiquette.

"He's the headmaster," she said correctly.

"Yes, but is he a good man?" She was about to object, but I went on. "I mean you told me that you loved a good man once. Is Mr. Tyson good like that?"

"No," she said without hesitation. "No, he is not good like that."

I think that even at this stage if she had been able to say 'Yes', I would have thrown in my hand. But she couldn't.

She hurried on: "Of course, in many ways he's an excellent headmaster; he insists on cleanliness, on the proper order. But he is given to rages and excesses, and sometimes it's difficult for a body to know where to turn."

It was she who gave me the resolve to tackle my role in the final act.

After lunch I got up and dressed. I didn't want to have to appear in pyjamas at the fateful meeting and I thought I needed some practice at being up and about again. I went down to Miss Daphne's sitting room and found her filling in forms in front of her fire.

"Are you feeling all right?" she said.

"Will you come with me this evening, Miss Daphne?" I asked her. "Please."

"I don't see how I can," she said. "Mr. Tyson hasn't asked for me to be present."

"But I'm asking you. He's going to expel me, you know."

"Expel you?" She was affronted.

"Yes."

"Why?"

Not for the first time, I told my story. I was prepared to leave out most of it, but she was a good listener and, after all, she was the Queen.

In the end she said, "Well I suppose I might be able to come. Not to say anything, of course, but I could take you there since you are under my care. But I won't say anything. I've got my job to think of, you know."

THE FALL OF THE KING

I was so pleased that I challenged her at dominoes. She beat me again and again.

The meeting was set for six o'clock.

At ten to six Miss Daphne took my arm and led me through the long corridors until we arrived at Tyson's study. No sound could be heard from within.

"I think we're early," she said.

Then behind us the front door that led to the car park opened and there was Tyson, with the Doctor and another man.

Miss Daphne rose to the situation.

"Headmaster, I've brought Yeoman here, as you asked, but he's still not fully recovered so I think it would be a good idea for me to stay with him."

In front of a visitor, Tyson was obliged to be gracious.

"Yes, of course, Matron."

And he ushered us all into that thick-carpeted Victorian lair of his where glasses had been set out on a table and extra chairs had been brought in.

I sat on the sofa, and Miss Daphne took a high-backed chair behind me. The doctor and the other man remained standing. When I got a proper look at the latter, I knew at once who he was: he was the Judge, the chairman of the governing board. He was an old man, older than Tyson, as old perhaps as Mr. Hodman, square shouldered and dignified in his movements, with thin grey hair brushed back over the crown of his head and over his temples.

THE FALL OF THE KING

He had a thick, bristly moustache that seemed out of place on so venerable a figure, and eyes that were energetic and kind.

Hadley had been right: he was the very picture of the Judge.

There was a quiet knock on the door, which, it seemed, I was the only one to hear. It was repeated, and Tyson went to the door and opened it. Hadley entered, paler than ever, and looking tiny. When he saw me on the sofa, he passed Tyson with only a mumble of politeness and came to sit by me. He reached for my hand and pressed it in his own.

"I'm so glad you're all right," he said.

The next knock was loud and confident. Tyson opened the door again, and this time it was the enormous Garth. He was like a tree, that man, but a tree lopped of its lower branches and, with them, of the gentler side of his nature. Tyson was clearly pleased to see him and ushering him in, introduced him to the Judge and the Doctor.

I got the impression that the Judge was rather puzzled, as if he couldn't see why Garth should be present.

But I knew that he was Thor, and that Thor had to play his part in the final act.

They stood around while Tyson served them with drinks. There was some attempt at small talk, which failed. Tyson looked at his watch.

"They should be here soon," he said. Then he took the governor by the arm and began telling him how the new science laboratories were nearing completion, and praising our recent sporting successes.

THE FALL OF THE KING

Doctor Fell was inspecting the bookcases. Garth, finding himself on his own and conscious of his awkward bulk, deposited himself heavily in a chair next to Miss Daphne.

There was another knock at the door, the last. In came my father, followed by Fred Avery.

My father is a short man, but he is not one to be easily awed, and he strode in as if there was business to be done and no good reason to delay it.

"Good evening," he said. "I'm sorry if I've kept you waiting."

He shook hands with Tyson, but to me he gave only a quick, meaningful glance. I read it instantly: he didn't like having to be there, and if I was really to blame he would not be merciful. But I also knew that he would be prepared to do battle with injustice. He has always been like that.

I looked at Fred, but he was watching the floor. He and my father both refused a drink, and so Tyson had to begin.

"The nature of this meeting,' he said, "is an exceptional one. There have been other times in my long – and, I hope, productive – tenure as headmaster of this school, when I have been forced to take action which I would have wished to avoid. And when there have been disagreeable measures to take, I have always borne the responsibility myself, without involving members of my staff or the parents of my pupils."

My father had extracted a cigar from his pocket, and was lighting it.

"However," Tyson continued, "in this case the dignity of the

THE FALL OF THE KING

school and my position as its Head have been threatened in an unusual and disturbing fashion. Please understand that I have already made up my mind how to deal with this threat. This is not a court hearing, but I have thought it proper that there should be witnesses to my sentence and that I should invite your open comments on it." He paused, removed his glasses and wiped them carefully on the hem of his gown. Then he pointed to Hadley and myself on the sofa. "These two boys," he said, "are to be expelled from this school for the practice of black magic."

It was, I must say, a startling way of putting it and it seemed to have the desired effect. I heard Miss Daphne draw in her breath behind me. I was watching my father. His eyes were narrowed and he looked very grim.

"I would have liked," Tyson went on, "to find another way of describing their activities, but there is no other that will suffice for the diabolical scheme on which they have been engaged. I need not trouble you with the details. Both Doctor Fell and Mr. Garth will support my account of the facts, and both of them will be able to tell you that what these boys planned was nothing less than the disgrace of the good name of the school and the overthrow of its headmaster.

"I apologise to you, sir -" here he turned to my father - "for bringing you to the school only to be given this deplorable news but, out of respect for your own integrity and sense of honour, I wanted there to be no doubt in your mind that my actions have been correct and above board. I hope I can spare you the details since they are of a particularly unsavoury nature."

Tyson was the only figure standing, his hands gripping the lapels of his master's gown. He must have felt very sure of himself.

The Judge cleared his throat.

"I'm afraid, headmaster, that we will after all require you to give us the details."

He was polite. He was even a little apologetic in his tone, but he was also very firm. I liked him instinctively; there was something about him that you felt you could rely on. He looked as if in other circumstances he could be a humorous man. He had extremely thick eyebrows as well as that vigorous moustache. His cheeks were a lively red and long years of smiling had scored deep friendly lines around his eyes and mouth.

"I don't understand, sir," said Tyson. The Judge was the only person in the room on whom he could not pull his rank.

The Judge rose slowly to his feet and walked to the fireplace. He motioned for Tyson to be seated. Again he cleared his throat.

"Mr. Garth, I should like first of all to satisfy myself as to the value of your evidence in this matter. You have been here only since the beginning of term, I believe?"

Garth shifted his long legs uncomfortably, straightening them and then re-crossing them the other way round. I could not see his face, but his legs lay there in the corner of my vision.

"Yes, sir, that's correct."

His voice was surprisingly tinny considering his huge frame.

"And so you cannot be especially familiar with these two boys in question?"

THE FALL OF THE KING

"Well, perhaps not familiar, exactly," he said.

"How well do you know them then?" said the Judge sharply.

I learnt later that this Mr. Westbrook was indeed a lawyer, and I reckon he must have been a pretty good one.

"Oh, you know," said Mr. Garth, trying his legs the other way round again. "To look at. Faces in the crowd, you might say."

"Faces in the crowd. Yes, I see. But the history of their crimes – you have been closely involved with that?"

"Oh no, I wouldn't say that, sir. No, not at all. I just came in at the end, you see. I've been, er, handy to Mr. Tyson a couple of times lately and he in turn has been good enough to confide in me." He must have looked at Tyson at this point, but if he was hoping for reassurance, he didn't get it. His only reward was a fierce glare from his boss which must have surprised him no end.

I knew what Mr. Westbrook was driving at and so, I'm sure, did Tyson. Garth had no business in the present gathering, but was simply providing moral support for Tyson – if moral is the right word. He was really a sort of bodyguard, and like most bodyguards he was more effective with his mouth shut.

His legs uncrossed again and were drawn up towards him. His big blunt fingers plucked at the knees of his trousers, hitching them up. His socks were a bright yellow.

He went on, trying to redeem his position. "Of course I'm pretty much aware of what's been going on. The boys I mean, the game, and that little scoundrel Tom." He stopped, but no one else was about to speak. Westbrook was waiting for him to say all that he had to say.

"Yes, the game in the woods with Tom, the way they'd been lying…" I had turned to watch him now. "That blighter Tom – he bit my hand, you know." And he held his hand up to be inspected by his neighbour, who happened to be Avery. Avery ignored it completely and for a moment it hung in the air like a piece of washing forgotten on a clothes line. There was an awkward silence. Then Garth withdrew his hand and abruptly got to his feet.

"I know when I'm not wanted." He made his way to the door. His parting comment was directed towards Tyson. "I'm afraid, headmaster, that you did not make clear to me what you expected of me this evening. I am sorry if I have disappointed you. Goodnight." And he left.

After a pause, the Judge addressed Miss Daphne.

"Matron, I'm sure you will understand if I ask you, too, to leave us." Miss Daphne immediately rose to go. "At the earliest opportunity I shall give you a full account of what happens here this evening. Thank you for coming." As Miss Daphne passed me, she leant down and whispered: "You know where to find me if you need me."

Thor and the Queen were gone. Everything was proceeding according to plan. It was strange how easily the initiative had passed from Tyson to the Judge.

"Now," said Mr. Westbrook, "It seems that only the principal actors remain."

He poured himself a drink and sat down next to the fire. "I'm not very happy about the position in which I find myself this evening. I once drove a Bugatti at Brooklands and I can tell you that that hot and greasy little seat was a good deal more comfortable than this." He actually did seem very uncomfortable. He loosened his tie and offered the bottle round. Avery accepted a drink, but Tyson sat straight up in his chair behind the desk, and his eyes held a glassy stare that I had never seen before.

The Judge then pulled some folded papers from his inside pocket. One of them fell to the floor between his legs and he retrieved it with a wonderfully swift motion.

"I have here two letters," he said. "The first is from Alfred Avery."

All eyes turned to Avery, who continued to sit watching the floor, a badge of red colouring his cheeks. He hated to be the centre of attention.

"In this letter," Mr. Westbrook went on, "which I received some weeks ago, Mr. Avery expressed the opinion that, at the time of the epidemic, Mr. Tyson was, in the eyes of most of the staff, endangering the health of the community by -" He looked at the letter, "'By an obstinate insistence that the school, under his leadership, must not be closed, contrary to the dictates of common sense and the advice of his nearest counsellors.'"

It sounded like a translation from Latin. Tyson glared venomously at Avery, but Fred was still looking at the floor.

My father had the next word. "Excuse me for interfering, Mr. Westbrook, but surely Mr. Tyson, acting with the advice of the doctor, was the proper judge of whether the school should remain open or not?"

"Perhaps we should hear from the doctor," said the Judge.

Dr. Fell decided on a performance. He got up and bowed slightly. I saw that Tyson had begun to relax, for here was an ally.

"It is my regrettable duty," said the doctor formally, "to give evidence that on medical grounds it was in the best interests of everyone concerned that the school be closed at the very outset of the epidemic and that all boys be returned to their homes."

Tyson was scowling.

"I advised the headmaster to do this, to close the school, from the very beginning." Tyson opened his mouth to speak, and closed it again. "But when he insisted, I had no choice but to carry out my duties as best I could. Perhaps I should have protested more loudly, but I did not then know the feelings of the staff, and, after all, I am a Doctor at this school, not an administrator." And he sat down with a satisfied glance around the company. It was almost as if he expected applause.

Hadley muttered something to me which I couldn't hear. I leant closer.

"Death got him," he whispered.

Tyson was badly wounded, but he was not dead yet. He rearranged a couple of papers on his desk, as if to re-establish himself, and I could see that he was preparing his reply.

"Before Mr. Tyson has his say," Westbrook went on, "I believe we should hear from the Deputy Headmaster."

THE FALL OF THE KING

Fred Avery pulled himself slowly to his feet. When he spoke he looked not at anyone in particular, but sideways out of the window, as if addressing the night air. His voice was quiet and gravelly.

"I'm sure we are all aware of Mr. Tyson's achievements," he said, "and for those we must applaud him. But perhaps only those of us who work in close and continual proximity with him are aware of his excesses, and in these we are obliged to try and restrain him. Of late he has become increasingly foolhardy and this episode of the epidemic is only the most recent in a series of misjudgements. That is my opinion."

And he sat down.

Tyson was watching him contemptuously.

My father intervened again. "We are losing sight of the matter in hand," he said. "I was asked to come here to listen to allegations against my son." He gestured in my direction, but did not look at me. He had not looked at me, in fact, since immediately after his arrival.

This was Tyson's cue. He, too, rose carefully to his feet.

"Thank you, sir," he said. "I am also of the opinion that minor complaints from members of my staff should be left for another occasion. What is at stake here tonight is a case of two boys calling on the powers of darkness to unseat their headmaster and bring disgrace upon their school. The instrument of their evil plan has been this game." He opened a drawer of his desk and took out my game. I had to resist an urge to leap up and grab it from him, as he exhibited it to his audience. I felt, rather than saw, my father stiffen, and knew that his eyes were on me.

Whether Tyson was aware that a mere board game did not constitute the kind of evidence he needed, or whether he was improvising I do not know, but before I could get to my feet, he opened the door of the stove and pushed the game into the flames.

"This should have been done a long time ago," he said, shutting the door. Through the glass I saw the flames suddenly flare up. And inside me a fire brightened and grew.

"I did not expect," Tyson continued, "that you would require any evidence but my own as to the nature and extent of these boys' maleficent practices. They have played this game many times, in spite of my clearest instructions to the contrary, with the sole object of defeating my authority."

Even Westbrook was silent. Tyson was exerting all the authority of which he was capable. The effect was alarming. His face was like some grotesque weapon, extended like a battering ram from his shoulders. His eyes bulged and glared, magnified by the lenses of his glasses, his chin was thrust out and his forehead gleamed. He turned to the Judge.

"Mr. Avery and Doctor Fell," he said, "have accused me of a misjudgement in the matter of the epidemic. They may have a case. But this difference of opinion can be discussed through the proper channels and at the proper time, and it can have no bearing on my decision to expel these two boys from the school. This decision will take effect immediately. I do not wish the boys in question to have the chance of subverting other pupils. I am sorry, Mr. Yeoman, that it should have come to this, and I hope you realise that it is a painful decision for me and one that I would have liked to avoid if only because of my personal regard for you. But I have never shrunk from my duty, and my duty in this instance is clear."

I think he must have believed at this point that he was going to get away with it. His judgement was greeted by silence. I thought my father might have defended me, or Pellinore, or even Westbrook, but Tyson was a fearsome creature in his own den and he had always treated the school as a personal fief. He did not surrender easily. You couldn't help admiring the man in a way: one of his witnesses was discredited, the other had turned against him, and yet he simply ignored these setbacks.

I knew that it was up to me now. I got to my feet. But the days in bed, and perhaps the enormity of what I was about to do, seemed to have drained the strength from my legs and I fell back on to the sofa.

Mr. Westbrook came to my rescue. "Ah, you have something to say, young Yeoman," he said kindly. "Don't worry about standing up, just tell me what's on your mind."

So I addressed him personally, as if there was no one else in the room. It made it easier.

"It's not true about the game, sir. It was just a game, sir, and Hadley and I never thought of doing anything but just playing it. I mean what *could* we do with a board game?"

Nobody had an answer to this. Mr. Westbrook urged me with a nod to continue.

"Somehow Mr. Tyson got the idea that there was something sinful about it. I don't know why. It was old, you see, and drawn by hand and there were some curious characters in it. If it hadn't been burnt, I could show you, sir, and you'd see that there was nothing in it."

Mr. Westbrook seemed impressed by this point.

"Yes, it would have been better if we still had the evidence," he said.

"But you can ask my father, sir. He knows the game. It used to be his."

This intelligence had them all listening. Even Tyson was taken aback, as I could tell from the rigid silence that emanated from his position behind the desk.

"And the doctor knows, too," I said, "because we played it together."

"Ah, you did, did you?" Westbrook turned to the Doctor. But I hadn't quite finished.

"And ask Mr. Avery, sir. Ask him to tell you that I had to go to his house at midnight to get away from the school."

"At midnight?" said Westbrook. "You crossed the road and woke Mr. Avery at midnight?"

"Yes, sir. You see he was the only one I could trust. Mr. Tyson was furious with me and had accused me of—well, you know what. And I had to tell somebody so I told Mr. Avery. I was very frightened, sir."

Tyson interrupted, shouting. "It's a pack of lies," he said, "a damnable pack of lies, and this boy -" he indicated me – "is a thief, a liar and…evil."

THE FALL OF THE KING

My father at last saw where his allegiance lay.

"That's enough, Tyson," he said. "You are Headmaster, but your authority does not extend to the vilification of my son in my presence. And you can call him a liar if you like, but think very carefully before you call me one."

He went on to confirm my story about the game. It had indeed been his, he said. The game was no more an instrument of the occult than Monopoly. Mr. Tyson had apparently been suffering from a gigantic misapprehension, and it seemed it was not an isolated case.

"There is no need for you to expel my son," he finished, turning and addressing Tyson directly, "because I am voluntarily removing him from this school as long as you are Headmaster. I shall advise Mr. Hadley to do the same. And to you, Mr. Westbrook, I recommend that the governors consider very carefully whether the school is in the right hands."

That was excellent. But there was more to come. Avery cleared his throat, but his voice sounded as deep and gravelly as ever.

"As Deputy Headmaster, I too would like it recorded that Mr. Tyson has become increasingly illogical and tyrannical in the exercise of his power. As to the boy's story, it is true. He arrived at my house in a state of some shock. His account was a garbled one, but there can be no doubt that he was suffering from a very real fear for his safety. My wife will confirm this. I am not clear, however, what part was played by the doctor in all this."

I had gambled on Pellinore's faith in me. Truthful to the last, he had not confirmed the lie I had told that it was Tyson, rather than the doctor, whom I had been fleeing that night, but he did not deny it either.

The doctor rose again and announced that he had no confidence in Tyson's judgement either in the case of the epidemic or in the matter of the game. He regretted that it had been he who had drawn the Headmaster's attention to the game, due to a misunderstanding of Hadley's delirious ravings. He had since satisfied himself that there was no truth in his original suspicions and had even insisted on playing it in order to be sure.

"The game was an interesting one, but no more than a simple board game. I would have conveyed this opinion to Mr. Tyson, but I felt he was no longer in a mood to listen to reason. In fact, as a Doctor, I have come to have serious doubts as to whether Mr. Tyson's mental equilibrium is adequate for the demanding nature of his responsibilities."

Attacked by the Merchant, Pellinore and Death in the First Kingdom, the Hangman found that even the King's crown was not enough to save him. His face was apoplectic, but the Judge gave him no chance to speak.

"In view of these serious allegations," he said, "of which I had already received some idea, I will call a meeting of the Board of Governors as soon as it can be arranged. Meanwhile I must, on my own responsibility, take the step of asking Mr. Avery to assume the duties of Headmaster until further notice."

THE FALL OF THE KING

I was watching Tyson out of the corner of my eye. The great red face had gone pale and he looked older. His fingers played nervously with the hem of his gown.

My father rose to leave.

"I am sure that you are acting rightly, Mr. Westbrook." He turned to me. "We'll leave now. Go and get your things," he said. "With your permission, Mr. Westbrook, I will try to get in touch with Hadley's father, who I gather was unable to come today for reasons of distance, and suggest that I take his son under my wing for a day or two."

"Goodnight, Mr. Westbrook, and thank you," I said.

Then I turned to Tyson.

"I'm sorry, Mr. Tyson," I said.

And we left.

CHAPTER FOURTEEN

THE GIANT'S GRAVE

I did not go back to school that term, nor did Hadley. I heard from my father that the governors had duly decided to relieve Tyson of his duties and had appointed Avery as his temporary replacement. The doctor, I learnt, had resigned his position at the school.

I met Mr. Hadley in London. He talked to my father, but we boys were not asked to be present at the interview. Mr. Hadley was a nice man, shy and pale like John, with long nervous fingers and the look of a man of learning, with the suggestion of a quiet and private depth behind his eyes.

Hadley had asked me if he could come and stay with me in Dorset and my father had agreed if Mr. Hadley gave his permission, which he did. Just after Mr. Hadley left, there was a telephone call for me. It was Tom.

"I'm coming back next term," he told me.

"That's great, Tom."

"But I'm on holiday until then."

"So are we. Hadley and I."

"Yeah, I know. They told me. Are you both going down to your place?"

THE GIANT'S GRAVE

"Yes."

"Can I come too?"

"I'm not sure. I'll have to ask."

"My parents say it's all right by them."

I made him hold on while I went and asked my father.

"The more the merrier," he said.

So it was agreed that we'd meet at Waterloo Station the next day. Platform 12.

Tom was there, wearing an army combat jacket several sizes too large for him.

"Where on earth did you get that?" I asked.

"Borrowed it from my father," he said with a mischievous smile that told me that the word 'borrowed' was not quite accurate.

Tom was very excited. I don't think he'd ever been out of Surrey before and the idea of real countryside sounded like paradise to him.

"Not too many buildings down there, then?" he asked me.

"Not too many."

"Ah," he said with satisfaction. "And not too many people, I don't expect."

"No."

"Ah," he repeated, with greater satisfaction than before.

And during the journey, while Hadley and I made plans for our fortnight of glorious freedom, Tom sat with his face glued to the window of the carriage and ignored us completely. Or not quite completely, because he did look up once. We had been talking about the doctor.

"He's still got the game, then?" Tom asked.

"Yes."

"Ought to get that back, you know."

We knew perfectly well, but we'd been trying not to think about it.

I wondered what my mother would make of Tom, how he'd fit into our household, but I needn't have worried because the fact is we hardly saw him. He was up before us in the morning and only came into the house long enough to bolt down his meals.

Hadley and I went fishing, took Brandy for walks and spent long afternoons with books and puzzles, but Tom was always off on his own, exploring and making traps. He'd spotted a mink on the river and had a big plan for trapping mink and selling them for coats.

I had written to Mr. Hodman asking if we could visit him, and received a prompt reply saying he was expecting us for 'a bite to eat and a ramble'.

Hearing that it was to be a longish expedition, Tom decided to come with us. We set off early. It was cold and the frost still lay crisp and white along the sheltered roadways, but the sunshine was brilliant.

When we reached Mr. Hodman's cottage, Tom refused to come in.

"I'll just have a look around," he said, "and find you later."

"But we'll be going off for a walk. You might miss us."

"Never mind, I'll find my own way back. See you this evening." And with a wave of his hand, he was off.

THE GIANT'S GRAVE

"But you don't know the way," I called after him.

Tom just laughed.

Mr. Hodman was, as ever, kind and attentive. We ate cheese sandwiches and baked beans but this time the beans were cooked.

"I asked my sister-in-law." he said, "and she told me that these things are not eaten cold."

They were pretty good on the outside, but they got colder towards the centre.

Hadley was very shy with Mr. Hodman, but I could see that he liked him.

After the washing up, which took us a minute or two longer this time – there being three plates, two forks, the breadknife and the pot for the beans to deal with – Mr. Hodman suggested a walk.

"Rather a long one, I had in mind," he suggested, "if that's agreeable to the two of you, that is."

It was.

I wanted to tell him about events at school, but he cut me short.

"I've had a letter from Mr. Westbrook," he said, "telling me of the outcome regarding your Headmaster."

Here was a surprise.

"But you don't know Mr. Westbrook, do you?" I asked him.

"Not personally, no," he said. "But I gather him to be a good man."

"But why did he write to you?"

"It was actually I who initiated the correspondence," he said.

"You wrote to *him*?"

"Yes. I hesitated about interfering, but I felt that at least some of what you had said should be presented to a competent authority. I found out that the Chairman of the Board of Governors was a Mr. Westbrook and I took it upon myself to write to him."

So this had been the other letter that the Judge had referred to.

"He had no good reason to believe me, of course, but I expressed myself quite carefully and I learnt from his reply that he did in fact know my name, from some trifling history that I wrote many years ago."

"Are you a historian, Mr. Hodman?" said Hadley, his curiosity aroused. "That's what I want to be," he added shyly.

"And a very good one you'll be, I don't doubt," said Mr. Hodman. "No, I'm not really a historian, but I've always interested myself in the remoter reaches of the past and, when I lived in Kent, I made a study of some of the local abbeys. It appears that Mr. Westbrook is also interested in these things."

"So he believed you."

"I have no way of knowing. But he respected my intentions and indeed he thanked me for alerting him to a situation which he would have wished to know of sooner."

There was one question I needed to ask.

"But what about the game?"

"Yes, the game. The game, I fancy, is one of those odd relics with a power for either good or evil, which were made made by men who knew a little but perhaps not enough, and all in all the last act of your headmaster is probably something you should be grateful for." He looked at me searchingly. "I don't expect you to agree with me, though."

I wasn't even sure of the answer to that question.

"You've been lucky, the two of you," went on, "I think you remember my advice to you from the beginning, Edward."

I blushed.

"Why didn't you give the game to Mr. Hodman, Edward?" Hadley asked.

"Oh no," Mr. Hodman laughed, "I wouldn't have accepted it. It's not in my line at all, that sort of thing."

"But," I insisted, "I don't understand how the game worked. Why it worked, I mean."

"You see, it is fashionable – 'scientific' is the current word – to deny the existence of powers in this world that can be neither seen, nor gauged, nor convincingly explained. For perhaps a million years man has lived on this planet, and he has not only accepted the existence of such powers, but he has spent a great deal of time propitiating them. Now we are told that all this was so much ignorant superstition. Never believe it," His tone was emphatic. "Never doubt for an instant that such powers exist. But as to the workings of them, well, it takes a deal more cleverness and determination than I can claim to understand that. In your game there was something of a...mythic force, I think we could say, and something of a family ghost and, perhaps, the evidence of some great design in which you may have a part to play."

"But why me?"

"Who knows how the instruments of Albion's purpose are selected? Or, indeed, what exactly his purpose is?"

"But surely Albion himself can't be the source of the game's power?" Hadley protested.

Hod walked to the window, and contemplated the view of the hills for a long moment.

"I think," he said, "it's time for us to make a move, as we've a fair way to go," and something in his tone convinced us that it would be fruitless to enquire further.

We climbed the hills to the south of the village, and I began to get an inkling of where we were heading. We passed the Dorsetshire Gap and came to Nettlecombe Tout, a little circular tump or tumulus fringed with stately trees, where Mr. Hodman stopped.

"In your game, it was this place that stood at the border of the Fourth Kingdom. And not without good reason, I feel. If you listen a moment, the trees may tell you something."

This suggestion did not seem at all odd to Hadley or to me. Mr. Hodman had a way of including all the mysteries of the world within the compass of his talk; or rather, because he treated everything as equally serious, there was no room in his vision for the superfluous. There was no coincidence in his world because everything had its proper weight in the design.

We stood and listened. It seemed that a special little breeze, that I had not noticed before, had sprung up around the circle of trees and set them moving. Their whispering was gentle, but solemn and very

THE GIANT'S GRAVE

ancient. A ripple ran along the short grass to where I was standing and I felt it run through me, as if for an instant I had become like a tree or a blade of grass. There was an indescribable loneliness up on that spot, and all I could think afterwards was that it had been, for a moment, as if we were not there. Mr. Hodman was gone, Hadley was gone, and I was no more than a pair of eyes. Gone were the villages and the roads, and all the traces of human history, and there was left only that solitary hilltop and the breath of an infinitely ancient language spoken by the breeze, the plants and the trees.

We didn't talk as we walked away. Our path led down to a farm and a few cottages set in a perfect little valley. A flock of sheep was spread over the lower slopes. The world was back, but it was still very old, very quiet. It wasn't until we reached the tarmac and the telephone cables, and a small red car whizzed by us, that our own century of mechanical madness returned.

We walked along the road for a while until we were under a grass-covered hill. A track led up and along the lower slopes. After a hundred yards Mr. Hodman stopped and sat down on a large slab of weathered limestone. Hadley and I sat near him.

"This is the Giant's Grave," he said.

I had guessed it, but I think Hadley was taken by surprise because he looked nervously around him as if something would spring at him from the undergrowth.

There was nothing to see, really: a bank that may have been an earthwork, a few old stones. The hills rose steeply behind us.

"Or Albion's grave, as I prefer to think of it," Mr. Hodman

THE GIANT'S GRAVE

continued. "Mighty old Albion, last of the race of giants, son of the sea itself, and for a time king of this land. But not like the kings of history, for Albion was a giant in stature and his memory was incredibly old, reaching back into the dimmest mists of time, when the Gods lived upon the earth. His learning derived from the Gods, and from the Gods he received his inheritance. Like a God he ruled this beautiful isle, and it was called the Island of the Blessed, for all that lived here were under his protection and under the protection of his elfin bands."

"But I thought Albion was stolen away by the elves," said Hadley.

"There were many Albions, John, many who were given the name of the giant, and the web of their stories has become so thickly interwoven, so many times told and forgotten and revived that they have become inseparable. But the Albion I speak of was the first, and his name means the 'all-good'. For you see the story of this island was begun in goodness and will perhaps end in goodness, and many, many are the people who have fought for it, but ever and again they have come up against those who have aspired for earthly riches and the dominion over men which is won by the sword. Warmongers and false priests enslaved the bodies and minds of Albion's children and enclosed them with walls of fear and there were few who escaped."

As he spoke his accent became more and more Welsh and his anger against the tyrants was formidable. But at the end he broke into a great, rich laugh.

THE GIANT'S GRAVE

"But all over the land are the secret memories of the past and the whispered promises of what was and what will be. And there are books and litanies and stories which cannot all be burnt, outlawed and suppressed. And every day children are born for whom the future cannot be laid out like a blank, black motorway, and each of those lives may be a statement of freedom."

We began walking back. I looked over my shoulder at the sight of Albion's grave: just a bit of a bank by a bit of a track by a road under a hill. The centre of the game.

We returned by the road. At the next village Mr. Hodman bought us a bar of chocolate and we sat and ate it outside the Post Office.

"Of course," he said, "the story I told you – like all stories, is only part of a longer story. The Giant's Grave has no doubt served at times as a kind of entrance to the underworld. I expect you've heard of such things."

"The Caer Sidh," said Hadley.

"Yes, indeed. I can see that you are already familiar, John, with certain stories of this kind."

Hadley nodded.

"Well, you know then that there are a number of barrows, tumps and the like which, according to the old Celtic beliefs, acted as entrances to the other world. Some of the great warriors of the past had occasion to knock on these mysterious doors and some no doubt paid dearly for their boldness. I think it altogether likely that Albion's grave may have been some such mysterious door and that is why it was given as the centre point of your game. It is the sort of place that a sensitive soul would do well to avoid at dusk."

We parted at the cross and, as we walked off, we saw Hod again standing with arms upraised in farewell or blessing.

Because I wasn't sure of the way home, we backtracked as far as a turn-off which I thought would take us up towards Bulbarrow. There was not much daylight left and a mass of clouds had blown in from the south giving a chill and gloomy character to the day's end, so I wanted to find the quickest way back.

We had gone only a hundred yards or so when we spotted a car parked in a gateway. A small red car.

"Hey look!" said Hadley as we approached it.

"Don't be silly," I said.

But when we got to the car, it was indeed the one that we wanted least in the world to see.

Our instincts were identical. We walked quickly past it without a word. Then we began to run.

We ran until we were exhausted and stopped, panting, in another gateway.

"Let's get out of here," said Hadley.

It was what I would have liked, too, of course, but I hesitated. To begin with, we couldn't be sure which way the doctor had gone. Perhaps he was ahead of us; perhaps he had already observed us.

But I also had a feeling that it was fated, this encounter. Ever

THE GIANT'S GRAVE

since my game with the doctor I had tried to avoid thinking about him, about what sort of devilry he might be up to with the game. I had no wish to dwell on the fact that it was really I who was responsible for whatever he might be doing. Tyson was defeated but the defeat had after all given me little satisfaction, because the doctor was still at large, still scheming. And our game was still in his possession.

It had never occurred to me that he would work out the geography of the game so quickly. But of course he would have studied the names, and he had the advantage of being a Westcountryman. In his obsession he would have puzzled over and nagged at the problem until he had hit on the solution.

And now I knew exactly where he was. He was at the Giant's Grave.

I told Hadley my thoughts. He didn't feel any braver than I did, but he agreed with me: we couldn't just run away.

We climbed the gate into the field and returned along the hedge to where the car was parked. I wished my heart wouldn't throb so hard. We looked carefully around before climbing back onto the road. Two rooks spotted us and flew out of an elm tree, cawing raucously. I wondered if the doctor could see them too.

Through the back window of the car we saw Hadley's version game. The doors were locked.

"We could break in and grab it," I whispered. "And then run."

But the doctor might be closer than we imagined, and there was the awful possibility that he would return and give chase. The

THE GIANT'S GRAVE

clouds had thickened and the light was gloomier than ever. We were far from home and in country that I didn't know.

There was only one thing for it: we had to go back to the Giant's Grave. Our main hope was to keep the advantage of surprise. We knew the doctor was around and, probably, where to find him. The track we'd taken with Mr. Hodman led to a point just above and behind the big stone slab, and there were some thick bushes which would screen our approach.

The closer we got, the greater grew my desire to turn and run, but just as I thought I wouldn't be able to resist the urge any longer, I heard a noise.

"Sshh!" I laid my hand on Hadley's shoulder and pointed. Then he heard it too. It was a harsh, scraping sound that stopped and started.

We felt a bit safer then. The doctor was already at the Grave, and he was up to something. As long as we could hear the sound we had nothing much to fear.

The scraping was of metal on stone.

"He's doing something to the slab," I whispered.

And then we saw him. We ducked behind the bushes and, ever so slowly, raised our heads.

He was crouched over the slab scraping the dirt from the edges. A pick-axe was leaning against a nearby tree.

The doctor stood up and said something aloud. For a moment I thought there must be someone else with him and I looked desperately around, but there was no one at all. He was talking to himself. Straining my ears, I could just about make out the words.

THE GIANT'S GRAVE

"A crowbar. I should have brought a crowbar."

He walked to where the pick was standing and carried it back to the slab.

"There must be a sign," he said.

A few minutes later he ceased his scraping and peered at the surface of the stone. Apparently he could find nothing, and anyway the light was fading fast.

Looking up he heaved a long sigh.

"Now is the time," he whispered.

He seized the pick-axe and began trying to insert the flat edge under the stone. For a while he couldn't find a purchase but once he had, he strained all his weight against the handle. I was sure he couldn't shift the stone, but I was wrong.

"Aah!" shouted Doctor Fell.

The last of the light was behind him and we could clearly see his silhouette against the sky. Keeping one hand pressed against the handle of the pick, he was scrabbling with the other on the ground behind him, evidently searching for a wedge. He picked something up and jammed it into the opening. Then he collected some more wedges and repeated the procedure a number of times.

Now, to our horror, he started coming towards us.

We crouched as low as we could behind the foliage. I hardly dared breathe and kept my head pressed against my chest, hiding my eyes. I could hear the sound of the doctor's feet among the leaves, moving a few paces, stopping, moving again. He was just beyond the bushes, only a yard or so away. Suddenly a branch that lay right between my feet began to move. I nearly yelled out. The branch slid slowly away from me into the blackness of the undergrowth.

"Fine," said the doctor. "Perfect." His voice was so close that I shook. Surely he must hear my heart pounding.

But the branch was being dragged back to the slab and I heard him starting to lever again. Cautiously I raised my head over the bush to watch. The sky behind him now held only the faintest glow and yet somehow I could see the doctor more clearly than before. Then I realised why. Above us the moon had emerged and it was full.

The doctor was busy with his levering, grunting with the effort. I could see that the slab had now been raised to twenty or thirty degrees.

Then there was another noise. Close to me, in the bushes to my right. I stiffened, and heard it again. A rustling, as of an animal. A rabbit? A fox? No, something bigger. A badger maybe.

The doctor had stood up, facing the moon. He raised himself to his full height and stretched out his hands towards the moon.

What happened next should have been funny, had it not been so macabre, for the doctor began to undress. I was trembling with cold and my feet and my fingers were numb, but Doctor Death was undressing. First his jacket, then his shirt, his boots, his trousers.

Underneath his clothes he was wearing a costume of some kind. Only his hands and face were pale in the light of the moon, but the rest of him was covered by a long, dark garment.

Once more he raised his hands towards the moon and murmured some words I couldn't hear but which had the monotonous quality of a chant. Then he bent over the slab and seemed to check or strengthen the support, before easing himself feet first through the narrow gap and disappearing.

Neither Hadley nor I moved for an incalculable length of time. Did one minute pass, or five, or ten?

Suddenly the rustling to my right was repeated. Whatever it was, was coming closer.

"Enjoying yourselves?" said a voice.

It was Tom. Who else?

"Tom, you scared me to death," I whispered. "How the hell did you get here?"

"Never had you out of my sight," he said casually.

"Sshh!" I pointed to the slab.

"What are you waiting for?" said Tom. "The rat's in the trap."

Hadley had joined us.

"Let's get out of here," he said.

"What do you mean?" said Tom scornfully. "We've got work to do. Come on."

And he stood up and started threading his way through the bushes. I don't think I realised what he had in mind, but I followed him anyway. When he was clear of the bushes he broke into a rapid trot in the direction of the slab. I came after, more cautiously. Hadley was right behind me.

The slab was half-open supported on a pile of flattish rocks and stones. A large rock had been wedged in at the other end.

"Come on," said Tom. "Take that one out, the big one."

THE GIANT'S GRAVE

There was no time to think, no time to consider. Tom picked up the pole that had been the doctor's lever.

"Your end first," he shouted.

I pulled out the big wedge, which was loose. Tom raised his pole and drove it against the pile of rocks at his end. They crumpled instantly under his attack and the huge slab thudded down like a big lid closing. There was still no sound from underneath. It was as silent—well...as the grave.

"*Now* let's go," said Tom.

"Wait. The car keys," I said.

But Hadley had already found them, in the doctor's jacket pocket.

How three frightened, breathless young boys arrived, running, at the telephone box in the nearby village on a night of full moon, may later have been told by certain curious onlookers, and may eventually have reached the ears of the Dorchester policeman who had received a very strange telephone call at exactly that time. Or maybe the lorry driver who picked those three boys up a little later on the road out of the village and gave them a lift as far as Okeford, may have mentioned this unusual episode to his friends. Certainly he would have wondered what the boys were doing there at that hour and why they were so unnaturally silent, and perhaps he noticed that one of them kept a small parcel hugged to his chest throughout the ride.

And the police who investigated the case no doubt scratched

THE GIANT'S GRAVE

their heads over the question of what had become of the keys to the little red car, having understandably failed to find them in the hedge, where one of the three boys had flung them.

But somehow the various clues remained fragments of an incomplete puzzle and no official callers disturbed the nervous quiet of those three boys as they refused to go out of doors for the next couple of days.

In Friday's edition of the *Western Gazette* they found this curious item:

> 'Following a mystery telephone call received at Dorchester Police Station at eight o'clock on the evening of March 22nd, police found a man trapped in an underground hollow in the vicinity of Melcombe. At first inclined to treat the call as a hoax, the police did not investigate the matter until the following morning. On raising the large slab which covered the hollow – apparently an old well or cistern – they found the man half-dead from the cold and from the extremity of his ordeal. He was taken to Dorchester Hospital where he is said to be physically recovering but apparently incapable of coherent speech or even of giving his name.
>
> The police believe that it is most likely a question of an eccentric potholer who has paid a high price for his foolhardiness, and want to take the opportunity of warning the public against such ill-conceived ventures into subterranean places.'

"It must have been a long night for him," Hadley said.

Also by Roger Norman:
RED DIE A Dorset Mystery
SHADOWBORNE